RESPECTING THE MAN
THE BOY WILL BECOME

RESPECTING THE MAN THE BOY WILL BECOME

A Parent's Guide to Loving, Teaching and Raising Teenaged Sons

Brother James M. Kelly, C.F.X.

Published by St. Xavier High School, Louisville, Kentucky
with the assistance of Butler Books, Louisville

ISBN 1-884532-30-6

Fourth edition October, 2003

To order books contact:
Saint Xavier High School Development Office
1609 Poplar Level Road
Lousville, KY 40217
502-637-8485

Acorn art on cover by Brian Smith, a student at St. Xavier

Editing by Irene Rapier

Published through the generous support of
Robert S. Allison
J. David Beneke
John R. Bohn, Jr.
Paul E. Buddeke
William S. Butler
Thomas O. Eifler
John L. Hoeck
Albert C. Horton
W. Barrett Nichols
W. Earl Reed III
Margaret C. Thomas

Dedicated with loving and fraternal gratitude
to the memory of

Brother Kevin Kenney, C.F.X.
and
Brother Ivan Corkery, C.F.X.

CONTENTS

FOREWORD

Over the past several years, many friends have commented to me on the power of Brother James Kelly's monthly letters to parents of teenage boys who are students in his school. Each message is filled with the kind of counsel a parent needs. Each is timely and so much on target.

My fellow Saint Xavier High School board members and I have been overwhelmed with the thought that we should assemble these great pieces of advice in book form. We believe the collection will provide much-needed direction to parents working so hard to raise their boys.

Fellow board member Bob Allison has spearheaded our effort to convince Brother James we should assemble these messages into book form. It has taken over a year of high-pressure selling to receive Brother James's reluctant permission to produce this book. The "straw" that finally produced an "OK" was our decision that any dollars generated by the sale of this book will go to the Saint Xavier Legacy Campaign.

I believe this book is a natural. Brother James's words are direct, and his great advice to parents of teenage boys is timeless.

—Robert L. Shircliff
Chairman, Board of Directors
Saint Xavier High School
Louisville, Kentucky

INTRODUCTION

In the spring of 1982, when I was preparing to become the Principal of Xavier High School in Middletown, Connecticut, I attended the convention of the National Catholic Education Association in Chicago. The convention was sponsoring a workshop for new principals. One of the speakers, a Brother of Holy Cross, who was the principal of a large all-boys high school, mentioned that he wrote letters monthly to the parents of the boys in his school. He felt that it helped to make his contact with the parents more personal. I thought that it was a great idea which I would like to adopt, but I didn't have any idea what to write about monthly to parents. There is only so much you can say about the annual card party and the procedures for P.T.A. night. Early in my principalship I met with a mother who was very much distressed about some very typical adolescent behavior which she had seen in her son. He was her first boy, and she thought that she might be seeing something abnormal. As she talked, I laughed. She was describing a typical teenaged male, and when I pointed that out to her, she was rather relieved. I decided then that I would help parents to understand how the typical teenaged male goes about living his life and finding his way to mature adulthood. Teenaged boys can, at times, be a mystery to parents, even to fathers who were once teenaged boys themselves. Over the years I have not seen that many changes in the nature of the teenaged male. Thus, while the metaphors in my letters change, the subject matter doesn't.

I have had the great grace to live for thirty-three years in the Congregation of Xaverian Brothers. The wonderful tradition of our Congregation and our "corporate wisdom" have given me the insight and the understanding I have needed as a teacher during twenty-five years and as a school principal and president during the last fifteen years. For over 125 years the rule of the Xaverian Brothers urged the Brothers always "To respect the man the boy will become" when dealing with their students. I've seen many boys grow into mature and productive men, and I've come to appreciate the wisdom of that admonition in the old rule. The content of my letters to parents reflects very much the corporate wisdom of the Xaverian Brothers.

As I mention in the first letter, I come from an Irish background, and I am very much an Irish storyteller. There is an old Irish adage that you should never let the truth get in the way of a good story! While all of my stories are based on fact, I play with the details to preserve anonymity and to ensure the smooth flow of the narrative. I hope you find my Irish storytelling helpful.

—Brother James M. Kelly, C.F.X.

ON XAVERIAN EDUCATION

I come from an Irish background, and because of that I am almost genetically incapable of making a point without telling a story. As I begin my tenure as President of St. X, I want you to understand something of my philosophy of education, and that requires a couple of stories. Please bear with me!

When I was in the last month of my principalship at Xavier High School in Middletown, Connecticut, where I had served for seventeen years, nine of them as principal, I received a call from a local drug rehabilitation clinic informing me that a former student of mine was a patient and that he would like to see me. I had taught him seventeen years before in 1974, but I hadn't seen him since the day he graduated. Of course I went to see him, and he told me the story of his life since high school and of his growing problems with an addiction to alcohol. Now in his mid-30's he was trying to put his life back together. We talked for quite some time, and as I was about to leave, I asked him why, after seventeen years, he had called me. He replied very simply, "Because I knew you'd come."

It would never have occurred to me not to go see him. As a young Brother starting out at St. John's High School in Massachusetts, I had the good fortune of living with a number of legendary Xaverian Brothers who taught me early on what Xaverian education is all about and how Xaverian Brothers deal with students. I recall one day the superior of our community, Brother Ivan Corkery, dispatching two young Brothers to the Worcester County jail to visit a St. John's boy who was in very serious trouble with the law. I can't remember if the young Brothers were objecting, but I do remember Ivan's response. He said, "Oh, you'll be sitting in the first pew proud as peacocks when one of your old boys says his first Mass. Well, in the pulpit or in prison they are all ours, and we don't abandon them in their need even when we can't possibly approve of what they've done. Now get!" In the years since I first heard Brother Ivan speak those words, I've thought of them often and tried to live out in the classroom and in my role as a school administrator what those words signify about Xaverian education.

In our educational philosophy the Xaverian Brothers have always emphasized the primacy of the student. The school exists to educate young men and to assist them on the difficult road to Christian adulthood. Boys don't learn to become men without a few good bumps and bruises. I've met very few boys in my career who actually learn from what their parents or their school teachers tell them about life. The school of hard knocks seems more to be the norm. That doesn't discourage me. I accept it as reality, and on more occasions than I care to remember I have provided some of the "hard knocks" which have proven valuable learning experiences for the young men involved.

If you'll pardon another story, in Connecticut the school's parent organization ran an ice cream booth annually at the county fair to try and raise funds. One afternoon as I was helping them scoop ice cream, a number of students whom I had expelled from Xavier wandered by the booth. All of them stopped to chat, and the parents were somewhat amazed at the cordial, friendly exchanges that went on between us. Now I won't pretend that every young man that I ever expelled from school still thinks of me fondly, but I would venture to guess that the majority do simply because, even as I dismissed them from school for very good reason, I tried to let them know that I hadn't given up on them as people and that I was taking the rather drastic step of dismissal because I was concerned about them. Sometimes hard knocks are the life raft that a kid really needs.

I am well aware that Saint Xavier has always been the measure by which the Xaverian standard of excellence has been set. Saint Xavier is the oldest Xaverian school in this country and the third oldest Xaverian school in the world. Our history as a religious community is intricately bound up with the history of this school. Maintaining and enhancing the Xaverian philosophy and influence in this school will be one of my focal points. Before I am anything else, I am a Xaverian Brother, and before this school is anything else, it is a Xaverian Brothers' school. As parents, your day-to-day interaction with the school will be with the Principal, Mr. Sangalli, and with his assistants. When I was considering the appointment of a principal, I chose Perry Sangalli not only because of his superb academic and professional qualifications but because he knows the Xaverian charism in education inside out and backwards and has lived it beautifully as a teacher and school administrator at St. X and at Mount St. Joseph in Baltimore.

Last week I asked a member of the faculty if he were a senior, and I recently got lost giving some alumni a tour of the building. On the one hand there is a great deal that I don't know about St. X, but on the other, there is very little that I don't know about adolescent boys and about the traditional values of Xaverian Brothers' education. The latter should stand me in good stead while I learn the former. If in January I still don't know where the band room is or who comprises the math department, then we can all start to worry!

ON WINSTON CHURCHILL

As parents, you have perhaps noticed that adolescent boys do not mature according to adult time schedules, nor do they share an adult sense of urgency about planning for the future. Each boy matures according to his own time schedule. Of course, he doesn't know himself what this time schedule is. Adolescent maturity has nothing to do with a conscious decision on the part of the adolescent. It just happens when it happens, and nothing you or I do or say is going to hasten the process. That doesn't mean that we shouldn't try, but we have to realize that our attempts probably do more to make us feel better than they do to make him mature more quickly.

Recently Mr. Sangalli and I were conversing with the mother of a sophomore who was concerned that her son just didn't seem to have a sense of urgency about anything, never mind his own future. While she was talking, Mr. Sangalli and I both began smiling. We school teachers have the dubious

19

distinction of never escaping adolescence (hopefully not our own), and the two of us have probably heard the same complaint from parents more times than we care to remember.

I'll never forget Mrs. Donohue who on one PTA night shook her son's report card at me and yelled, "I'm too old for this." The poor woman was working on her third and last son, and he had chosen a different time schedule from his older brothers, one of whom was a doctor and the other an accountant. She was afraid that son #3 was on his way to becoming a derelict. I told her to do what the British do: Remember Winston Churchill.

A superlative speaker, a magnificent writer and a charismatic leader, Winston Churchill was certainly one of the greatest statesmen of this century and largely responsible for England's surviving the Second World War. Yet, Nobel prize winning writer that he became, he was not much of a student during his younger years. In fact, his school reports caused his parents continual anxiety. In June of 1890, his mother wrote to him at school:

> ...Your work is an insult to your intelligence. If you would only trace out a plan of action for yourself and carry it out and be determined to do so — I am sure you would accomplish anything you wish. It is that thoughtlessness of yours which is your greatest enemy.

Churchill's school performance was such that he was not qualified to enter a university. He was, however, accepted at Sandhurst, the English Military Academy. When he heard of his son's acceptance at Sandhurst, Lord Randolph Churchill wrote to him:

> ...There are two ways of winning in an examination, one creditable the other the reverse. You, unfortunately,

have chosen the latter method, and appear to be
much pleased with your success. The first extremely
discreditable feature of your performance was missing the infantry, for in that failure is demonstrated
beyond refutation your slovenly happy-go-lucky,
harum-scarum style of work for which you have always been distinguished at your different schools.

This "slovenly happy-go-lucky, harum-scarum" boy grew into
a magnificent statesman, writer and orator, the savior of his
country! And a magnificent example of the time honored tradition of the "slovenly" schoolboy who ultimately lands on
his feet.

I couldn't begin to enumerate for you the number of
times I run into some of my "old boys" who seemed destined
in high school for rather useless lives but who have become
successful men with happy families and promising careers. I
remember one boy who drove me crazy when he was in my
junior English class. Focusing on anything for more than two
minutes was a real trial for him, and I spent ten months trying
to keep him in his seat. He scraped by with a gentleman's "D,"
and I assumed that he would never get into, never mind make
it through, college. Recently I met him again, looking like a
million bucks in a three piece suit, a successful business man
with a happy family. We had a nice chat, and he commented,
"You thought I was going to be a bum, didn't you, Brother?" I
had to admit that I hadn't held out much hope for him in high
school. He just laughed and said, "You always told me that
someday I'd have to grow up. Well, I did. I just took a
little longer than most in doing it." He's just one example.
I could give you hundreds.

Never underestimate the ability of the "slovenly happy-
go-lucky, harum-scarum" schoolboy to land on his feet.
You may never rid yourself of the gray hairs he has given
you now, but be comforted by the fact that he will grow up

despite present signs to the contrary. One day, when all your prodding, nagging and hollering have paid off, you will look back on his high school days with a different eye. Then, while you play the doting grandparents, you can sit back and watch his kids drive him crazy!

As for Mrs. Donohue — well, her son went on to become president of the school in his senior year, was accepted at and graduated from a fine college, and bumpy beginning not withstanding, seems to have landed on his feet.

ON 1963, 1993 AND HAPPY PARENTS

"If a teacher does not love his or her students
and their immortal souls, then the teacher might
as well be frying hamburgers for a living."
          —Sister Mary Madelon Morris
          A retired Sister of St. Joseph
          and former teacher of the President

Although it was thirty years ago, you probably remember just where you were when you heard that President Kennedy had been assassinated. I was sitting in Sister Mary Madelon's junior English class at Marian High School in Framingham, Massachusetts. When the announcement came over the public address that Kennedy had been shot, the principal ordered the whole school to produce their rosary beads and to begin praying. In that pre-Vatican II era, every student in a Catholic school carried a pair of rosaries for just such a crisis (and for identification in case of an accident—they'd know to call a priest before a doctor!). In unison, 900 teenagers began the rosary, and we were not very far into it when the announcement came that Kennedy had died. It seems to me, as I look back on it, that his death was one precursor of the end of an era.

In the Catholic world of 1963, Catholic parents normally sent their children to Catholic schools. This did not represent an incredible sacrifice since Catholic schools at the time were driven by "nun and Brother power" which made them rather inexpensive to operate. At St. Xavier in 1963, Brother Edward Daniel, the principal, had 34 Xaverian Brothers working in the school, and the tuition was $200.00 per year. The enrollment was 1,379, and these boys came to St. X almost automatically from the very strong Catholic grammar school system in the city. Brother Edward Daniel didn't have to worry about recruitment. He was probably more concerned about dealing with the angry parents of boys whom he had to turn away.

We opened the 1993-1994 school year with 1,337 boys, a figure comparable to the enrollment of 1963. There are now, however, only 7 Xaverian Brothers on the faculty, and I don't need to tell you the tuition. You are more aware of that figure than you would probably like to be. Choosing a Catholic education for your children is now much more of a sacrifice for you than it was for your parents a generation ago, but despite that sacrifice, you have made a choice.

In the years since 1963, the important things about St. X have remained the same. Gospel values are still the firm cornerstone on which we attempt to build a boy's education. Excellence remains the hallmark of the school. Whether it be in an extraordinary number of National Merit Scholars or in a superb athletic program, St. X challenges its students to strive always for excellence. Of course, we have facilities now that students in the early 60's probably couldn't even have imagined, but we only have the facilities because so many people believe in the value of a St. X education.

Why, you might ask yourself, is Brother James telling us all of these things which we already know? Well, there is one thing that has changed since 1963. Brother Edward Daniel had the post-World War II baby boom to rely on for students and the Catholic world view which strongly encouraged Catholic parents to put their children in Catholic schools. The post-World War II baby boom is over, and Catholic children do not now automatically attend Catholic schools. Given these realities, St. X puts a great deal of time and energy into the recruitment of students. We must be successful since we opened school this year with more students than we opened last year, but at times I wonder if we aren't getting a little too glitzy. I have always believed that the best advertisement for a school is happy and successful alumni, happy parents and happy students who are being challenged to become the best they can be. When it comes to happy and successful alums, St. X seems to have the market cornered. There may be some unsuccessful and unhappy St. X alums somewhere, but I haven't met any of them. The students here are a remarkably happy group of young men, given the normal ups and downs of adolescent life. As for the parents, well, I leave that up to you to decide.

If you are, however, a happy parent, if you feel that your investment in a St. X education for your son has been worth the sacrifice, then please spread the word. Happy parents are our best recruiters and our best ambassadors in the greater Louisville community. If you know a young man who would benefit from a St. X education, please encourage him and his parents to explore St. X. Although finances will always be a consideration, during this school year we distributed close to $500,000 in financial aid to 350 young men. Thanks to the generosity of our alumni and our many friends, we are trying to keep St. X available to all young men, economic backgrounds notwithstanding.

About once a week I make a "Presidential Progress" throughout the school, stopping in classrooms just to see what's going on. When I finished that progress today, I went into Mr. Sangalli's office to tell him how incredibly impressed I am with the quality of instruction that I see going on here. Since I'm the "new kid on the block" and can take no credit for the superlative school that St. X is, I think I can make a rather objective assessment. We don't have any teachers here who would be better off frying hamburgers for a living. The Xaverian Brothers may be in the minority on the faculty, but the Xaverian spirit in education is still alive and well. We have 85 men and women on our faculty who truly love their students and who are passionately concerned about their immortal souls. I don't think parents could ask for much more than that from their sons' teachers.

I don't remember much of what Sister Mary Madelon taught me. I do remember how much she and the other nuns were concerned about our success as students and, more importantly, as people. I have listened to many alums of St. X reminisce about their days here or on Broadway. Many of the stories involve some Brother throwing an eraser at them (wooden ships and iron men and all that!), but through all the stories it is clear that these alums realize how much the Brothers cared for them and how concerned they were about their success. That still goes on at St. X, and it is worth every penny of the tuition you pay. Please feel free to tell the world about it!

26

ON DEATH AND FAITH

Last week I had the sad experience of watching two parents bury their child. In my teaching career I've been present at far too many funerals of young people. This seems such an absurd inversion of the natural order of things. How can God possibly allow something so painful? I have yet to hear a decent explanation, and this letter certainly isn't meant to give one. The death of a young person is a real test of faith for me, but perhaps such occasions are the times when faith is really faith with no possible help from reason.

Years ago when I was in college, I became quite sick, and the doctors felt that, in all likelihood, I would not recover. I remember very little of the critical point of my illness, but months later when I was well again, the doctor told me that I had made only one coherent comment during that critical time. Apparently the doctor told me that he was going to let my parents come in to see me. For the first time in days, I focused on what was being said to me and rather forcefully (so they tell me) told the doctor that he was not to allow my mother to see me in the condition I was in because it would hurt and upset her too much. Needless to say, the forces of hell could not have kept my mother out of that hospital room.

I have often thought that perhaps the most painful part of the crucifixion for Jesus must have been the pain of knowing how much his mother was suffering watching Him die. When Mary held Jesus's dead body in her arms on Good Friday afternoon, I doubt she was thinking about the joy of an Easter Sunday. In the intensity of her pain, she probably had some very angry questions that she wanted God to answer for her. Perhaps even after she had her Son back on Easter, she must have wondered how God could ever have allowed such suffering and pain in her life and her Son's.

We have in Jesus a God who has become man and who knows first hand the pain of suffering and death. At those times in our life when we cry out, "God, it hurts!", our God responds, "I know; I've been there." Perhaps that's the only answer we can expect from God to those very difficult "Whys?" It's not such a bad answer when you think about it. Perhaps faith is only really faith when it's all we're holding on to.

ON TIME, ATTENTION AND A (MORE THAN OCCASIONAL) HUG

Donna Reed is dead, isn't she? One might ask if she ever really existed. I'm speaking about Donna in her role as mother *par excellence* in that extraordinary family on the "Donna Reed Show." My mother never cleaned the house in a cocktail dress nor was she as even tempered as Donna, so I and many other early "baby boomers" like me grew up wondering why our families just didn't quite measure up to Donna's. I don't doubt that ideal parents are just about as rare as ideal children. With over twenty years in education I've seen glimpses of ideal parents, and I've thought at the time that if these parents could just bottle their recipe, they could make a fortune and save many other parents a great deal of trouble. The main ingredients of the recipe seem to be time and attention. To this I would add a more-than-occasional hug.

     Years ago, in fact at least fourteen years ago, I was

sitting in my classroom giving make-up work. Report cards had been distributed on that day, and one of my "make ups" was whining that he was going to run away from home since his father was going to kill him as soon as he saw the report card. Mid-whine one of the other students in the classroom got extremely excited and started yelling at the whiner. "You should thank God your father is going to kill you. You should be happy he cares enough to look at your report card. My father won't ask to see mine. He won't yell at me if it's bad, and he won't pat me on the back if it's good — which it is. You should thank your lucky stars that your father's going to yell." The "whiner" was very much taken aback and so was I. Of course, I made some attempt to defend the boy's father, but the kid shot back, "Don't bother, Brother. He just doesn't care, and you can't make excuses for him." Fourteen years later I remember the scene and the conversation vividly. I think I remember it so well because the boy was in such pain, and I was so powerless to do anything about it.

Teenaged boys would lead you to believe that what they most want from their parents is to be left alone. They'll be embarrassed if you pay them a lot of attention, and they'll tell you that it doesn't matter if you spend much time with them. They will pretend that they want to crawl under a rock if you hug and kiss them, particularly if you do this while others are present. They will also pretend that all they want from you are material things, new skis, a CD player, a car or whatever. If you believe them, then, of course, you have violated Kelly's first law of dealing with adolescent boys: never take what they say or do at face value. Rarely will a kid tell you what he really needs and what he really feels. Frequently he doesn't know himself. He could be heartbroken that you didn't show up for his baseball game or his performance in the school show or (believe it or not) the night his parents are supposed to meet his teachers, but he'll lead you to believe that he couldn't care less.

More than he needs anything else, a teenaged boy needs to know that he is loved. Much as he will protest to the contrary, he'll not come by that knowledge by the material things you might give him beyond the basics of food, shelter, clothing and a good education. He needs to know how important he is to you, and you just can't communicate that with "things." The next time you want to give your son something to show him that you love him, skip the CD player. Give him your time, your attention and a hug. He'll probably snarl at you and demand the CD player. He won't mean it, and he'll never admit that you've given him what he really wants. But trust me when I tell you that, despite his protests, you will have given him what he wants and needs most, and you will be teaching him how to go about being a good parent when the time comes.

Donna Reed and the Brady Bunch aren't the norm for family life. Real family life is much messier, far less neat. At the end of December, the Church celebrates the Feast of the Holy Family. It's rather easy to forget that the Holy Family started out with an unwed teenaged mother and a poor (probably teenaged) carpenter who had to take care of a son who wasn't really his. Mary and Joseph had very little to give Jesus beyond their time and attention. And no doubt more than a few hugs. Forget Donna Reed and the Brady Bunch! Give your son your time, your attention and a daily hug, and rest assured that God will then take care of whatever else is lacking.

ON IRISH WAKES AND
PARENTAL PRIVILEGES

There's an old story about a good Irish lady who had just lost her husband. As she sat at the wake surrounded by her children, the local pastor waxed eloquently about the deceased, touching upon his sobriety, his generosity and his total commitment to his family. As the good priest went on canonizing the deceased, his widow became visibly distressed and quite anxious. At one point she turned to her oldest son and exclaimed, "Glory be to God, it's the wrong wake we've come to. It can't be your father he's talking about. Go up and see who's in that coffin."

At one of the opening meetings of the PTA this year when you came to hear about your son's academic program, I commented to one group (I think it was the junior parents) that I am incredibly impressed with how polite St. X students are. The words were no sooner out of my mouth than I saw all sorts of quizzical glances in the eyes of the assembled multitude. Whose kids is he talking about? Certainly not my son! Polite? What is he seeing that I don't see? You've probably heard the old expression "House devil, street angel." The expression probably applied to the Irish widow's husband, and in some way it applies to all teenaged boys. Very frequently what you see at home in your son is not the face that he presents to the world, but you certainly shouldn't let that discourage you. Actually, it's a parental privilege for which you should be most grateful.

If your son has begun dating, you might be surprised to discover that his girl friend's parents think that he is prince charming. He's never surly to them, but of course, they don't have to live with him. He doesn't have to rely on them for parental permission, and they don't control his purse strings. It's easy to be prince charming when there's no real cause for conflict.

Most teenaged boys have a very healthy sense of survival, and they know what they have to do to get by. In school (particularly at St. X) there are very clear expectations and very clear consequences for not meeting those expectations. Add to that the adolescent need to be liked, and we at school normally see the better side of your son, the smiling side, the polite side, the industrious side. And we get to send him home to you at 3 PM every day!

You are perhaps wondering how I can say that it is a parental privilege for you to see the darker side of your son's personality when the world sees a side of him that you'd very much enjoy experiencing more frequently. Well, it's quite simple. Last month I told you that more than he needs anything else, a teenaged boy needs to know that he's loved. When you see his darker side, you are reaping the rewards of doing your parental job of making him secure in your love. He's not too sure about the world and how it will judge him if he shows some of the more negative sides of his personality, but he feels free to show them to you because he knows that there isn't anything that he can do, no matter how horrible, that will make you stop loving him. You may be furious with him. You may ground him. In a worst case scenario you may even threaten to throw him out of the house, but even "tough love" is still love, and he knows that. In a very real sense you've given him the security that comes with love, the security of a safe harbor free from the buffets and storms of a world which to an adolescent can seem at times very threatening.

A few years ago when I was principal in Connecticut, we had a brief period when three of the fathers of members of our junior class died within two weeks. The reaction of the other young men in the class was very telling. The father-son relationship is at best tricky, particularly during the son's adolescent years, and there can be a great deal of very normal father-son conflict during those years. When the three fathers died within the two-week period, we saw a very strong reaction among the other members of the class, a reaction that was marked by anxiety, fear and some regret. That three of their classmates could lose the security of a father within two weeks brought home very forcefully to the other students how much they depend upon their parents and how little they appreciate them. Like most adolescent reactions, it didn't last very long, but for one brief moment we had two hundred young men who had a proper appreciation for their parents and for the love and the security which their parents give them.

One of the young men whose father had died quite suddenly came to see me a few weeks after his father's death. I had spoken with the boy before his father's death about their rather turbulent relationship. The young man was very upset because he felt that his father had died without knowing how much the son loved him. I assured him that his father did indeed know how much he loved him despite their conflicts. "But, Brother, I was so nasty to him. How could he know that?" "Because," I replied, "he was once a teenaged boy himself."

If you are very lucky, your son might tell you occa-

sionally that he loves you, but don't be bothered if he doesn't.
It isn't the teenaged thing to do. The next time, however, that
he's giving you a really hard time, remember the Irish widow
and thank God that your son feels safe enough and loved enough
to show you the less than perfect side of his personality. It
really is a parental privilege.

Let's pray for one another.

ON SNOWBANKS AND
INSTITUTIONAL HUMILITY

There is an old biblical adage that pride goes before the fall, or, in my case, pride goes before the collision. During the recent catastrophe of the snows here in Louisville, I made the unfortunate error of boasting that I, with my wintry New England background, knew how to drive in snow and that most Louisvillians did not. Shortly after making this boast I not only collided with, I flew into and on top of a monumental snowbank at the corner of Breckinridge Lane and Taylorsville Road. My encounter with the snowbank occurred at 7 AM at the height of rush hour, and as the sun rose grayly over Louisville, my little Geo Prism sat precariously on top of a dirty mound of snow in the turning lane of the intersection. After the car settled, only one of my car's wheels was touching the ground, and in the split second between the collision and the settling of the car on top of the snowbank, my only thought was that my sister was really going to be furious if I and my father died within a month of one another. Once I realized that I was not going to be killed, my second thought was that I wished that I had been injured at least a little bit because I was going to take great grief from the faculty and student body at St. X when they heard that this snow-skilled New England driver had met his match with a Louisville snowbank. My second thought proved correct. After the police arrived and the wrecker pushed my car (remarkably undamaged) off the snowbank, I arrived at St. X to find a bucket of ice and snow on my desk. Clever comments abounded, and lunch in the faculty dining room was a lesson in humility that I'll never forget. I've never had much difficulty admitting my mistakes, and I decided that I would turn my learning experience into a learning experience for the student body. During my Monday morning "Fireside Chat" to the school, I described my encounter with the snow and the lesson in humility I had learned. I suggested that the student body keep the adage "Pride goes before the fall" in mind and that they also learn to keep a sense of humor about themselves. Perhaps they can learn from their President's mistakes!

Even before my chilly encounter with the snowbank, humility had been on my mind, but I had been thinking of humility in institutional rather than personal terms. When we were planning this year's Open House for eighth graders, we were very much aware that in previous years St. X had not presented itself at Open House as the warm and welcome community that it is. On the contrary, the school seemed to give the message, "We are St. X. We're the best, and if you have any sense at all, you'll come to school here or send your son to school here." Definitely lacking in humility! It sounds like a school heading for a collision with a snowbank.

Fortunately the attitude I describe above is not really

prevalent at St. X. While there might have been a touch of hubris to our Open House presentation a year ago, as a school we are well aware that pride goes before the fall and that humility is a virtue we want to cultivate. St. X could not have survived, never mind flourished, over the past 130 years if it had not been continually evaluating itself, addressing its weaknesses and making plans for its improvement. Institutional humility. It's been part of the Xaverian charism in education since the day our founder, Theodore James Ryken, sent the first Brother into class over 150 years ago.

At one point in its proud history, St. X trained clerks for the Louisville & Nashville Railway. During the 1920's and 1930's our commercial department flourished under the direction of the redoubtable Miss Driscoll whom Brother Placidus, the principal, had to get permission from our Superior General in Belgium to employ since she was not a man. Miss Driscoll taught shorthand, bookkeeping and typing to St. X men, who became the clerical backbone of Louisville businesses. Yet even as this commercial department flourished, some wise Brother saw a snowbank looming in the roadway ahead and realized that St. X needed to change its direction if it were to meet the changing educational needs of its students. That institutional humility is still the order of the day here, and it's what you are paying for with your son's tuition. You want this school constantly to re-evaluate itself and to anticipate the skills your son is going to need for adult life in the new millennium. The document "Towards the Year 2010: A Vision for the Future" which the Saint X faculty developed last year is a wonderful example of the school's attempt to adapt to the changing world which your son will face in his adult life.

On his good days, when he's not whining about the amount of homework that he has or the fact that Mr. Stewart made him shave before he could go to class, your son is probably very proud of the fact that he's a student at St. X. He's in good company. There's a long green and gold line of 15,000 living alumni of this school who are proud that they attended it and who are grateful for the education it gave them. Tradition like that might be proud, but it is not built on arrogance. It's built on humility.

In the annals of Xaverian history, Brother Paul Van Gerwen, the founder of Saint Xavier, is always referred to as "that gentle apostle of charity." Superlative teacher and marvelous administrator that he was, Brother Paul was revered by his Brothers in religion for his saintly humility and his gentle charity. Please pray with me that Brother Paul's spirit will remain alive at St. X and that St. X will always have the humility to question what is in order to envision what might be.

Now, does anybody know why they leave snowbanks in the middle of turning lanes here in Louisville?

ON RUNNING AWAY, GOOD FRIDAY
AND EASTER SUNDAY

She was incredibly distraught. Her son had run away, and nobody seemed to know where he was. The standard line that he
would be back when he was cold and hungry was not helping.
In the midst of her grief, there was a brief moment of anger.
"He has the luxury of running away. Doesn't he know the countless times I would like to run away from home but can't because I have to be responsible? How would he feel if his father
and I just took off because we weren't 'happy.'" Running away.
It's an adolescent luxury we adults can't afford. Kids run away
from so many things, but mostly they run away from whatever
makes them unhappy, be that school work, a parental restriction, a real or imagined personal limitation, a family problem
or responsibility. If a teenaged boy put as much time into whatever it is he has to face as he does into looking for the easy way
out, he would probably find life a much smoother experience.
But, unfortunately, looking for the easy way out is an adoles-

cent strong suit. The Constitution of our nation tells him that he has a right to pursue happiness. The media, however, tells him that he has a right to be happy, all the time and without exception. It's a silly expectation, but he hasn't lived long enough yet to know that. This expectation, of course, leaves us adults with the grim task of thwarting his attempts at taking the easy way out and of blocking his efforts at running away. He thinks that we're killjoys. We know that we're only trying to get him as realistically ready for adulthood as we can get him.

In one scene in Enid Bagnold's relatively unknown play, *The Chalk Garden*, the two main characters Mrs. St. Maugham and Miss Madrigal discuss the merits of fertilizer. Mrs. St. Maugham wants to use a strong fertilizer on her garden, but Miss Madrigal wisely reflects, "Extract of humus is too rich for summer biennials. Don't pep up the soil before birth. It leads them on to expect what life won't give them." Obviously the garden becomes symbolic of life, and interestingly enough, the main conflict between Mrs. St. Maugham and Miss Madrigal is the raising of Mrs. St. Maugham's sixteen-year-old granddaughter who is a very troubled young woman. I had to teach this play once to seniors in a course not of my own devising, and although the play was a hit on Broadway and in the West End of London, I can't say that it had the same effect on my students. The play has remained with me, however, and has become for me a metaphor of the educational process and, *ipso facto*, of the parenting process. Your job and mine is to get your son as realistically prepared for life as we can get him. We do him no favors if we lead him to believe that life is going to hand him things that he hasn't earned or that life is always going to be fair. When these realities begin to dawn on a young man, running away can be an understandable reaction. And who among us would blame the mother I mention above for wanting to join her son in flight?

We began Lent as the Church has done for centuries

with the Gospel of Jesus' temptations in the desert. The theologians tell us that Jesus' temptations were the devil's way of getting Him to take the easy way out, to "cash in" on His divinity and to avoid the pain of His humanity. Jesus firmly rejected the temptations, accepted His humanity and faced the pain that being a human being entailed. Jesus knew that the cross would overshadow His life, but more importantly, He knew that the resurrection would triumph over the cross. That fact is so difficult to understand and so easy for all of us, adults and kids, to forget.

The boy did come home when he was cold and hungry, sorry for the pain he had caused his parents. He had discovered that running away solved nothing. It's a hard thing to run away from yourself. The Easter season is perhaps a good time to help our sons and students realize what our Lord learned during his forty days in the desert—that it is impossible to live life without "the cross." We can't avoid it, and it is probably less painful to face the cross than to attempt to run away from it.

In the pain of Good Friday, Jesus knew that there would be an Easter Sunday. That knowledge did not make the cross less painful, but it certainly gave meaning to the pain. The Easter season is a good time for life lessons and for faith lessons. Without Good Friday there is no Easter Sunday, and without Easter Sunday there is no resurrection. And without the resurrection, as Saint Paul reminds us, there just isn't much point.

May the good Lord bless you and your families with a very happy Easter.

ON THEORY AND PRACTICE

Be patient with all things, But first of all with yourself.
                                        —Saint Francis de Sales

Humility. It's a virtue essential to any adult who has to live or work with adolescents. If we were not already more than cognizant of our failings, we have our sons (or students) always willing to point out for us any discrepancy between our theory and our practice. Don't tell junior he drives too fast if you have a lead foot yourself. He will undoubtedly point out to you the double standard, and he will do it at the most embarrassing of all possible moments (for example, when you are having your boss over to dinner). I once recall telling a boy in a very angry tone to watch his temper. To this he immediately and justifiably replied, "Watch yours!" "Do as I say and not as I do" just doesn't cut it with adolescents, and that fact makes life all the more difficult for us adults.

A few years ago I was speaking with a father who was feeling rather guilty because he had difficulty following the advice which I so freely dispense in my letters to parents. His comments to me triggered my own guilt since on that very day I had totally lost my cool with three seniors whom I had intended to treat quite reasonably. Unfortunately, as I was attempting to provide a reasonable but firm response to their misdemeanor, one of them gave me "the look." You know the look. It's that face your son puts on which says quite clearly, "You poor pitiful adult. You know nothing. I, at the age of seventeen, know more than you ever will." The look is frequently accompanied by a surly "yea" in response to whatever question you have been asking. Either "the look" or the "yea" is guaranteed to propel me into orbit, and into orbit I went with these three seniors. I threatened them with suspension, expulsion, the police and anything else that came into my mind. They, with that sense which adolescents have when they realize that they have gotten themselves in over their heads, immediately began to grovel and to apologize profusely, claiming that they had never intended their original offense nor the Irish fire storm that was presently raging around them. Distressed that the whole interaction had not gone according to my plan, I sent them out of my office and took fifteen minutes to calm down. When I called them back, round two went pretty much according to my original plan. I was firm but reasonable, and they were repentant. The seniors left as if nothing had happened. I went home with a splitting headache.

Adolescents have an uncanny knack for backing adults into corners. Try as we might, it is rather difficult to be reasonable from a corner. If you find that at times (maybe more times than you'd like), there is a dichotomy between your theory and your practice when you are dealing with your son, I wouldn't worry too much about it. Look upon these occasions as a chance to practice humility. Above all, keep in mind the words of St. Francis de Sales: "Be patient with all things, but first of all with yourself."

ON JUG AND ETERNAL PERSPECTIVES

In a school as old as St. X, "tradition" is one of the hall-marks of the school, and perhaps one of the oldest traditions at St. X, certainly as old as our tradition of academic excellence and far older than our tradition of athletic excellence, is the tradition of JUG. Jug is the Xaverian word for detention, and it stands for "Justice under God." Of all the St. X traditions that exist, I would probably get the most grief from alumni if I even thought about tampering with the tradition of Jug. Not to worry! I'm a firm believer in Jug, and I applaud the fact that we have kept it at St. X in its pristine form with the boys standing for their time in detention. Recently members of the class of 1943 came to St. X to present Mr. Sangalli with a plaque which memorialized the time that their class spent in Jug down on Broadway over 50 years ago. I find it very interesting that their fond memories of St. X include their memories of time spent in Jug.

Frequently I wander into the Jug room after school just to see who's there. Jug perfectly reflects the school community, and the passing parade of "jugees" includes the entire range of St. X students. In one row there's the very bright but absentminded boy who forgot to put on his belt, while in another row there's the young man who just can't seem to get himself to school on time. There are those who have forgotten to have forms signed, and those whose adolescent exuberance has gotten a bit out of hand. Finally there are also those "lifers" who seem to make Jug their permanent home. As I pass through Jug and look at the blank faces staring at the back wall of room 119, I am often struck by the fact that these jugees will one day be running Louisville. Many of the most influential men in the Louisville community, doctors, lawyers, CEO's, CFO's, have all stood in this classroom or in a comparable classroom in the old school on Broadway and stared at a wall. I know one esteemed member of our Board of Directors who did more than his fair share of time in Jug in the late 1960's when Brother Corby Dufry was disciplinarian. I have no doubt that many of the young men whom I see in Jug everyday will go on to become as successful and as influential as have many of the men who have preceded them in Jug.

Parents occasionally ask what the purpose of Jug is, and some parents, obviously not St. X graduates, have even been so bold as to suggest that we might find some more positive punishment than Jug. But why tamper with success? Jug does two things which every school boy hates: It wastes his time, and it's boring. We rarely take kids out of Jug to do work because with "Jug labor" you get what you pay for and because work would reduce the discomfort of Jug by giving the young men something to do. The whole point of Jug is to impress upon the student that actions have consequences. You have probably realized by now in your dealing with your son that you have to draw very clear lines for adolescent boys and that you have to let them know what the consequences of crossing those lines are. Not holding a boy responsible for crossing the line is perhaps the worst thing that a parent or school teacher can do. The easiest way to lose control of a teenager is to let him know that you don't really mean what you say and that there aren't going to be consequences for ignoring the rules that you have set down. For those of us in the school world, Jug very adequately provides the consequence for the transgression and the re-enforcement that transgressions have consequences.

Let me give you an example from my own sad experience. During my first year of teaching, a year that most teachers will tell you is absolute hell, I had a class of juniors in a religion course entitled "Love, Sex, and Marriage." Besides the fact that as a 24-year-old celibate I was on very shaky ground with the subject matter, I had absolutely no control of the class. Although I had four other classes that went very well, this one class of juniors drove me to distraction, and they did it every day during the last period of the school day. At the suggestion of the headmaster, one of the older Brothers took me under his wing and assisted me in gaining control of this class. He very quickly surmised that my problem was that the boys didn't take my authority as their teacher seriously. "You're not communicating to them that you're in charge, that you're going to draw the line and that they are not going to cross it." "How do I do that?" "Stop making idle threats! Set down your classroom rules and stick to them." The situation with this class began to improve but so slowly that I was almost not able to perceive it. Unfortunately, in late April I jeopardized my progress by very stupidly threatening that I would keep them after school for an hour and a half the next day if they continued to misbehave. Misbehave they did, and I was in the proverbial corner. That night, after chiding me for my stupidity, my mentor re-enforced what I already knew, that I was going to have to keep the class after school. "If you back down now, you've lost them for the rest of the year." Of course, I had to tell the headmaster that I had boxed myself into this foolish corner and that he was probably going to have some very angry parents on his hands the next afternoon. Fortunately St. John's High School was very much like St. X. It was very old, and many of the boys' fathers had graduated from the school. For many of them a Brother's word was law even if the Brother was very young and very wet behind the ears. I kept the class until 4 o'clock, and from 2:30 until 4, they glowered at me while I pretended to do work and not to mind their sullen stares. When 4 o'clock arrived, I dismissed them, and surprisingly they left in good humor even saying good-bye to me as they went. That's one of the most delightful things about working with teenaged boys. They just don't hold grudges. I even saw in a number of them a grudging respect for me that I had stuck to my word. I didn't have any trouble with them for the rest of the year.

St. X is a rather strict school. Given the amount of energy and adrenaline that is present in this building every day with 1350 young men, we have to be strict, or we would lose control very quickly. As I mentioned above, teenaged boys don't hold grudges, and when they graduate from school, all of their experience at St. X passes into myth. The myth gets colored as the years go on, and to listen to the alumni talk at reunions you would think that their class went through the school when only the strictest teachers were here and when the disciplinarian was a hound from hell. The rule of the Xaverian Brothers which was in effect until 1965 admonished the Brothers always to "respect the man the boy will become." In God's good time boys do become men, and men frequently take an "eternal perspective" on their boyhood experience. When I hear present St. X students complain about Jug or the strictness of the school, I don't worry much about it. I know that twenty years from now they are going to be boasting at their class reunion about the hours that they spent in Jug, and if they have sons at St. X at the time, those young men will have to listen wearily to their fathers go on about how strict St. X was "when I was a boy."

Obviously you can't establish Jug as a part of your family life, but if you want to come through the summer in one piece, I do suggest that you take a page out of St. X's book and set down some very firm guidelines for summer behavior and stick to them. A 130-year tradition can't be that far off base, and, believe me, it will save you a few gray hairs. He's yours for the summer. I'll pray for you!

ON THE XAVERIAN CHARISM AND BOYS BECOMING MEN

We Xaverian Brothers are very conscious of our history, and in our Menology we have a brief biography of every Brother who has died in the Congregation since we were founded in 1839. Recently as I was glancing through the Menology, I discovered the entry for Brother Michael Feeley which mentions Brother Michael's unique way of answering the telephone when he was stationed at St. X. He would greet any caller with, "St. Xavier's— Send us a boy, and we'll send you a man." The Brother who wrote this entry about Brother Michael was recalling the man's sense of humor, but in a very real sense, he captured the essence of Xaverian education. We have been facilitating the growth of boys into Christian manhood for the last *155* years. The task is a formidable one, but we have a wonderful tradition which gives direction to all our efforts.

In early June, Brother Thomas More, Principal of St. Xavier from 1953 to 1960 and a teacher here from 1940 until 1949, was honored by the class of 1944 on the occasion of their 50th anniversary of graduation. In his address to the class Brother Thomas More articulated beautifully the approach that the Xaverian Brothers have taken over the years to molding boys into men, and I would like to share with you a portion of his remarks:

Finally, they were the years peopled by a community of teachers who called themselves Brothers. And crowding in on your memory are the faces of a Brother

- Who saw a talent in you even though you didn't;
- Who challenged you to think;
- Who helped you to understand things are not always quite what they appear;
- Who carried the message that new life emerges in death's midst;
- Who altered your perspective on the world around you and within yourself;
- Who introduced you to a world and a way of life whose horizons stretched you and caused you to grow;
- Who knew that what you needed desperately was the attention of someone who tried to see the world through your eyes and would not dismiss or trivialize your experiences just because of your youth;
- Who never gave up on you because it was his vocation to serve you and to love you.

I think I speak for all these Brothers when I say that I am grateful to God we were part of your lives during those heady and sometimes confusing days of your emerging manhood, when teacher met pupil and formed a bond that ties them together in an enduring fraternity.

Brother Thomas More was speaking of the days when there were forty Xaverian Brothers manning the classrooms at St. X, but the reality he describes, the bond between teacher and student, is still very much a reality here at St. Xavier. If there is one thing we Xaverian Brothers have done well as our numbers diminish, it is communicating our spirit and our philosophy of education to the wonderful lay men and women who collaborate with us in our ministry and who daily incarnate in the classrooms of St. Xavier the Brothers' tradition in education.

Every time I hear a student complain that a teacher or a coach is pushing him intellectually or physically beyond what he *thinks* his limits are, every time I see a teacher devising new strategies to get the boys to think, every time I see a teacher challenging a boy to change his perspective by not letting him take the easy way out, every time I see a teacher go to bat for a boy with another teacher or with the administration, every time I see a teacher or a counselor listening patiently and with sincere interest to an adolescent story that they've heard 10,000 times before, I know that the Xaverian charism in education is alive and well at St. Xavier.

Of course, you recognize that the Xaverian charism in education bears a striking resemblance to sound parenting. For 155 years the Brothers have collaborated with the parents of our students in facilitating the growth of their sons into Christian manhood. You know that your son will not succeed in life if he doesn't push himself beyond his limits or if he always looks for the easy way out. You short circuit his natural desire to play Peter Pan, the boy who never grew up, and you accept the whining which is the normal teenage boy's response to the discomfort of growing up. Even as you challenge him, you try to support him and to let him know how very important he is to you. That's the tightrope that parents and teachers walk when dealing with adolescent boys.

Recently I spent a very enjoyable evening with eight men from the St. Xavier class of 1929 as they celebrated the 65th anniversary of their graduation from St. Xavier. I listened in awe as they put names on the Brothers who did for them exactly what Brother Thomas More described in his talk, men like Brother Aloysius Wiseman (the principal whom they called "Big Al"), Brother Benjamin Burke, Brother Josephus Nolan, Brother William Sheehan and Brother Terrence Kilderry. These members of the class of 1929, all of whom are in their 80's, are still very much conscious of the role that their teachers at St. X played in forming them into Christian men. The overriding sentiment of the evening was, "The Brothers were tough on us, but they cared."

When I listen to the alumni of St. X talk about teachers who supported and encouraged them at a very important time in their lives and when I watch the young alumni return so frequently to visit with their teachers and to share something of the direction that their lives are taking, I know that the communal wisdom of the Xaverian Brothers, that wisdom which has helped generations of school boys become productive men, has found a home in the St. Xavier faculty. If Brother Michael were alive today, he could still answer the phone at St. X, "Send us a boy, and we'll send you a man." Please pray that it will always be thus!

Are you ready to send him back to school?

ON DRUGS, ALCOHOL AND
"THE NATURE OF THE BEAST"

Every other year I make a point of writing to parents about the difficult subject of substance abuse, and because we saw a marked increase in substance abuse during the last school year, I felt that it would be good to make this letter one of the earlier ones in this school year. While alcohol remains "the drug of choice" of most teenagers, the use and abuse of other controlled substances seems to go in cycles, and we now appear to be in a cycle when drug abuse is on the upswing. Last year we contacted the police because we were concerned about what we were seeing, and the police informed us that the use of controlled substances other than alcohol was definitely on the rise among a broad spectrum of students in the metropolitan Louisville area. They saw a major increase in the problem after spring break, and so did we.

Experimentation is an adolescent strong suit. Perhaps that's why adolescent boys do so well at laboratory sciences. This propensity to experimentation is not confined to the classroom but extends to all aspects of a kid's life. He will experiment with his car, with rules and regulations, with his parents' patience, and, unfortunately, with drugs and alcohol. Such experimentation is part of "the nature of the beast" and not necessarily a cause for parental panic even when it extends to alcohol and drugs. Abuse of drugs or alcohol, while not necessarily a cause for panic, should, however, be a cause for strong parental concern. In my experience with boys and substance abuse, it has frequently been the case that the parents are the last to know. I do not want you to become overly suspicious of your son, but I do want you to be aware of the possibility of problems. He's a kid, and kids can get in over their heads so quickly and so easily that parents would do well to keep their eyes open. Consider what follows as a variation on my rule of thumb: Don't be surprised by anything, but keep your eyes open so that you won't be surprised.

Predisposition: If there is a history of addiction in your family, then, obviously your son is more at risk than a boy whose family has no such history. This is nothing of which you should be ashamed. It's simply a fact that has to be recognized. Boys who are going through the social or emotional problems which are so much a part of adolescent growth and development are also ripe for problems with drugs or alcohol since these provide a quick, although brief, oblivion from the pain of growing up. Seniors who have been model citizens can see alcohol or drugs as a means of letting loose after all those years of being a "good boy."

Money: I can't emphasize enough that if your son has a bank account, you should be a cosignatory on the account, and you should monitor his cash flow. If he has a job, you should know how much he makes and where it goes. I know what I'm talking about here, and I know a good number of parents who mightily wish that they had heeded my advice on this point. You could discover that there is no money in your son's account at the same moment that the principal or the police are informing you that he has a problem.

The Late Night Blues: The wee hours of the morning provide nothing for an adolescent but an opportunity for trouble. Drugs don't make kids as sleepy as alcohol might. Curfews should not be just a summertime ground rule, and there definitely should be a prom night ground rule.

Sleeping and Eating: One lunch period in our cafe would confirm that most boys have bizarre eating habits, but if you see a marked change in your son's eating habits, you should be concerned. If he naps at odd times or if his sleep cycle changes, there is room for concern as well. Any marked personality change, abrupt mood swings, significant changes in grooming or hygiene habits and the like could be an indication of an abuse problem.

Friends: You should know who your son's friends are, and it is always good to get to know his friends' parents. You certainly have a right to object to the company he's keeping. Two cautions here. Your objection could have the opposite effect from what you intend, making him closer to the friends. In regard to his friends, you can't judge a book by its cover (trite but true), particularly when it comes to adolescents. Some of the nicest kids look as if they could be kingpin druggies, and some of the kingpin druggies look as if they could be on the cover of *Gentleman's Quarterly*. And vice versa!

School: We will do whatever we can at St. X to help a boy with an addiction problem, BUT once he brings his problem onto the school property, he puts himself in serious jeopardy.

An Atmosphere of Trust: It may strike you as contradictory to all that I have said above when I tell you that your best bet to avoid an abuse problem with your son is to keep the lines of communication open and to keep an atmosphere of trust in your relationship with him. There's no contradiction here. It's the tightrope that you as parents have to walk. If your son feels that he can be honest with you (understanding that his honesty may have consequences), you stand a good chance of nipping any abuse problems in the bud. Drug and alcohol abuse should be a regular and frank topic of discussion between you and your son. If you suspect that there are problems, talk with him. Unfortunately, like alcoholics, teenagers with abuse problems are masters of deceit. If you are still uncomfortable, talk with one of his counselors. They are here to help.

And Pray: Imagine your son quoting to you the words of Arthur in Tennyson's *Idylls of the King*:

> More things are wrought by prayer than this world dreams of.
> Wherefore, let thy voice rise like a fountain for me day and night.

I don't know how the parents of a teenaged boy could ever be atheists. How could you possibly get through your son's adolescence without God? Keep your eyes open. Don't be panicked or surprised if there is a problem. Pray for him, and, while you're at it, pray for me and for all of us at St. Xavier.

P.S. I am sorry that this letter lacks my usual humor and penchant for stories. The topic just doesn't lend itself to those techniques.

ON POLISHING DIAMONDS IN THE ROUGH

In my prior life as a high school principal, when I had to be far more concerned with school discipline than I do now as a school president, I developed **Kelly's Policy on Legal Mishaps.** In Middletown, Connecticut, the local paper published weekly the names of people who had been arrested in the town and occasionally pointed out when those arrested were students at the local Catholic high school for boys over which I was presiding. I often wondered if the paper and the public thought that attendance at a Catholic high school automatically turned a boy into a saint incapable of making a mistake. My policy on legal mishaps required that a student at Xavier inform me if he had gotten into trouble with the local constabulary before I read about it in the paper. I wanted to be able to cut off the locals who couldn't wait to tell me about a Xavier boy in trouble by saying, "Yes, I know all about it. The young man and I have already discussed it." In most instances, I would make sure that the young man had the proper legal advice, and I would usually write a character reference for him since ninety-nine times out of one hundred the boy really was a good kid who had made a stupid mistake. The students at Xavier were very diligent in response to my policy, and after every vacation or school holiday, I could count on a line of students waiting to tell me of their latest disasters.

On one occasion, however, the police were quicker than the students. They arrived at school to arrest two young men, members of our rifle team who had pointed a shotgun at a passing school bus. Although the shotgun was not loaded, the children on the school bus and the bus driver didn't know that. I couldn't prevent the police from arresting the two, but I was determined that they were not going to leave school without me, so I rode with the two young men in the back of the police cruiser. One of the arresting officers had had sons at Xavier while the other officer was very young and not terribly experienced. The younger one wanted to put the boys in handcuffs, but the older officer overruled him saying, "You obviously didn't attend a Catholic high school. These two might run away from us, but they won't run away from the Brother. They'll do whatever he tells them to do." Off we went to the police station, and I dutifully wrote character references for my two riflemen since they really were good kids.

Acting impetuously and without thought of the consequences is an adolescent strong suit. If teenaged boys took one minute to think of the consequences, they would probably not get themselves into some of the scrapes they do, but boys just don't think. That's part of the nature of the beast. When confronted with the consequences of their actions, they respond truthfully, "I just didn't think." If you were raised in the pre-Vatican II Church, you are aware of the three conditions for serious sin: serious matter, sufficient reflection and full consent of the will. I've never had trouble writing character references for young men in trouble because, quite frankly, I don't look at their difficulties in moral terms. A young man might do something that is seriously wrong, but sufficient reflection and full consent of the will are rarely present. Of course legal authorities don't care about this Catholic hair-splitting, and the young man can be very much legally responsible for what he does. I know that there are many teenagers in trouble with the law who really are on a moral low ground, but apart from a few adolescent drug dealers, I haven't encountered many of them in my career. I do, however, know a lot of "good kids" who just didn't think.

Because of my experience, I am a great believer in making a young man face the consequences of his behavior. The only way that a teenaged boy is going to learn not to act impulsively and to think before he acts is by suffering the consequences of acting impulsively and without thinking. Most of the time the scrapes he'll get himself into are "small potatoes," but facing the consequences now will help him to realize that it is necessary to think before he acts and that actions have consequences. It is a natural parental reaction to protect your son from the consequences of his mistakes, but, take it from a man who has sat in police stations more times than he cares to remember, the only way a boy is going to learn to become a responsible man is by realizing that his actions have consequences and by facing these consequences. He needs to learn this during his adolescence when the stakes are relatively small. I'm sure you've noticed that at St. X we are rather rigorous about holding the young men responsible for their actions and omissions. That strategy is part of the corporate wisdom of the Xaverian Brothers which I've been telling you about. There's a whole chapter in the book of Xaverian wisdom entitled "On polishing diamonds in the rough." Diamonds in the rough require a few healthy cracks with a chisel to smooth the rough edges and to bring out their inherent beauty. Your son will survive the polishing process and so will you. If the corporate wisdom proves true, as it has been doing for the past 155 years, you and your son will both be rightly proud of the man he will become when the polishing is done.

P.S. You may notice that I sing the old "Teach him to be responsible" tune rather frequently. In my business it's a song that never goes out of the top ten!

ON ADOLESCENT ENTHUSIASM
(AND THE JOY IT CAN BRING TO LESS
ENTHUSIASTIC ADULTS)

Come with me for a walk on a crisp fall day about the St. X campus. School has been over for 45 minutes, and the "sugar shack" in the cafeteria is about to close. Perhaps it's the sugar in the ice cream, cookies and soft drinks which they have been consuming, but the 50 young men in the cafeteria appear to have remarkable energy and don't look at all as if they had just put in six grueling hours in school. Remarkable energy! Remarkable enthusiasm! While St. X is vibrant and alive with academic energy during the school day, the school comes alive in a new way at dismissal, and it is in our extracurricular program that we see adolescent enthusiasm at its best.

The air is crisp but not chilly, and the breeze is strong enough to rustle the leaves remaining on the trees and to blow them about the athletic fields. The main field and all of the practice fields are alive with the football teams and the grunts and groans of over 200 boys as Coach Glaser, Coach Bean and their cohorts put our footballers through their paces. Blocking and tackling, these young men are putting 110% into the practice with probably a bit more enthusiasm than they tackled the law of cosines in trigonometry or irregular verbs in French during the school day. Over the groans of the football team waft the dulcet tones of the marching band as they practice the "Pirates of Penzance" on the lawn outside the Ryken House. As the band marches through their routine for the fourth time this afternoon, three of the elderly Brothers from Ryken House watch all of the activity in their backyard perhaps remembering the many years they spent in classrooms and on playing fields damming the flood of adolescent energy.

The cross country team and the soccer teams are just now leaving the locker room and jogging around the school and across Poplar Level Road for their practices in George Rogers Clark Park. They run to practice so that they can run at practice! There is nothing sluggish in their step, and you would think that this is the beginning of the school day rather than the end. As I walk back towards the school, I come upon a group of young men in the parking lot preparing to leave. It's the Tiger Chorus, and they have just had an hour's practice after school with Mr. Knoop to put the musical touches on the upcoming school liturgy for the Feast of All Saints. Disappointed that they weren't in perfect pitch for the practice, they hope that in the days remaining before the liturgy they will experience perfect harmony.

Back in the building, jug is just being dismissed, and 30 young men who have been staring somewhat glazedly over the past hour at a wall are more than ready to go home. Even the "jugees" display remarkable life and enthusiasm given their occupation of the past hour. In the foyer of the Driscoll Building there is some sign of a diminution of energy as a few young men catch a catnap while waiting for their parents to fetch them, but even a number of these young men are already beginning their homework and preparing for the next day's classes.

Through the foyer I hear Ms. Tingle at ten decibels hollering "Stage right" to her Thespians as they prepare for the November production of "Inherit the Wind." The auditorium is bustling with activity as Ms. Tingle directs the actors while stage and sound crews prepare the environment for another spectacular St. Xavier production. Here in the auditorium the sounds of girls' voices add a delightful touch to the normally baritone atmosphere at St. X.

The scream of a whistle and the sound of over 100 pairs of running feet echo from the gymnasium as basketball tryouts begin for another year. Once again Coach Bergamini has a bumper crop of potential hoopsters, far more than he can ever keep on a team, and by the look on his face, he knows that he's going to have to break a few adolescent hearts by the time he has assembled his team. The thought of cuts, however, has not deterred this gym full of St. X men who are only a portion of those who will ultimately try out for the basketball team.

The word enthusiasm comes from two Greek words which mean "filled with God." As I walk around St. X during the day and particularly after the school day, I am often overwhelmed by the enthusiasm of the St. X student body. They are indeed "filled with God" and a wonderful reminder to an at times less than enthusiastic adult of the reason for St. Xavier's existence. How many times have you been exhausted just watching your son's enthusiasm, and how often have you felt perhaps older than you are because you are so painfully aware of the contrast between his energy level and yours? Both you and I spend a good amount of our time curbing adolescent enthusiasm and channeling it in positive directions, but there are times when it feels good just to sit back and marvel at this enthusiasm. Occasionally we just have to thank God that He has put this wonderful energy in the young, and perhaps we can dream of the great things that these young men will do with all this energy and enthusiasm. Adolescent enthusiasm is definitely contagious. I may feel tired before I take one of my strolls about the St. X campus, but I never feel tired afterwards. I feel energized and grateful for the privilege of working with so many wonderful young men who are indeed "filled with God."

ON ST. AUGUSTINE, BOYS AND CARS

On a snowy winter night twenty-two years ago, I was driving the St. John's High School basketball team from the state basketball tournament in Springfield, Massachusetts, back to the school in Shrewsbury. Driving the school's bus was one of my least favorite occupations, but in those days it was the school policy that only Brothers could drive the bus. I lived in dread of notes from the athletic director assigning me this duty. The Athletic Department had an unwritten rule that if a team lost, the young men had to keep silence on the way back to school to ponder their mistakes, and since I left St. John's twenty years ago, I can now admit that I used to pray that the boys would lose whatever contest they were involved in so that the bus would be blessedly quiet on the ride home. I can't remember if we had won or lost on this particular evening, but the bus was very quiet, partly because it was quite late and partly because there was quite a storm raging outside. I think the boys had an instinctive sense that they had to give Brother Bus Driver a break with the noise if they wanted to arrive back in Shrewsbury in one piece.

The bus had a standard five-speed transmission, but that night, traveling at a speed not beyond thirty-five miles per hour, I never got out of third gear. As we crept along and I glared out into the snowy darkness, we were passed by a black car which was traveling well beyond the speed limit and dangerously fast for the road conditions. Inwardly I cursed the bloody fool who could take such a chance on such a terrible night. Shortly thereafter as I was peering out into the darkness, I saw something in the road ahead and slowed the bus to a crawl. It was the car which had recently passed us, and it was sitting in the middle of the road on its roof. Putting on the emergency flashers, I approached the car very cautiously, and as I drew the bus up next to the car, my heart sank as I saw four bodies in bright red St. John's High School jackets, motionless in the wrecked car. Yelling for the coaching staff to come with me, I hurried off the bus just as other passers-by were taking the young men out of the car. Seat belts were not in vogue in 1972, and I doubt that the four young men were wearing them, which makes it all the more miraculous that they lived through the wreck without any major damage to themselves. The car, however, was totaled.

Boys take to cars like ducks take to water. Unfortunately in taking to cars boys frequently use them in dangerous and inappropriate ways. Cars can somehow become a test and a sign of virility for an adolescent. With typical disregard for life and limb and with that false sense of immortality which the young have, a kid can drive like a maniac endangering himself and others, feeling all the while that he is in perfect control of the car and that he is not endangering himself, his passengers or any other unfortunates who happen to be on the road at the same time. Why does a boy have these perceptions of the situation? Simple. He perceives things in this way because he has no proper appreciation of his inexperience as a driver and he has absolutely no sense of his own mortality.

As the years go by, you and I become more and more aware of how little we know and how paltry our experience is. As the years go by, you and I become more and more painfully aware of just how mortal we are. Not so with a teenager. He knows it all. His experience is vast and far more insightful than that of we poor relics of a bygone era. And death? Well, that's what happens to other people, not to him.

Do you remember the story of Saint Augustine on the beach? St. Augustine was wandering on the beach trying to formulate some rational explanation of the Holy Trinity (God only knows why Augustine felt compelled to do this). As he walked, he came upon a boy running back and forth to the sea with a pail. When Augustine asked the boy what he was doing, the boy replied, "I'm trying to empty the sea into this hole I've dug in the sand." Augustine advised the boy on the impossibility of his tasks. The boy (he had to be a teenager) responded, "I'll put the sea in this hole before you ever understand the Trinity."

You and I will probably understand the Trinity before we ever convince our sons and charges that they do lack driving experience and that they are mortal. Yet hard as the task is, we have to try. The possible consequences of not trying are too terrible to contemplate.

A car is not just a means of transportation for a boy. A car is a symbol of his growing independence. From his sixteenth to his eighteenth year very little is going to mean more to a boy than his license and his driving privileges. In fact, depriving him of car and license is perhaps the greatest punishment a parent can concoct. You're not just depriving him of a means of transportation, you are depriving him of his new-found independence. The problem is, as with new-found anything, boys don't always know how to handle this independence, and they end up abusing it.

Talk with your son about the responsibility which goes with his driver's license. Let him know your expectations of his driving habits. If it comes to your attention that he has been driving recklessly, please don't hesitate to punish him. Take the car keys and keep them for a good long time. Yes, he'll be angry for awhile, but anger is always a better alternative to death. Encourage him always to wear a seat belt. I've known too many boys who didn't live to be men because of something as simple as a seat belt.

If you talk to your son about his driving habits and his responsibilities as a driver, he might think you're just one more adult on his case, but then again, he might just listen, and that might just keep him alive. Discussing the whole issue of driving with your son is one more impossible task for you to perform, but you're used to impossible tasks. After all, you decided to have kids, didn't you?

ON SAINT BENEDICT AND MIXED SIGNALS

When I was principal in Connecticut, I worked very closely with Sister Mary McCarthy, the principal of Mercy High School, which was less than a mile away from Xavier. Since there were no other Catholic high schools in the area, we functioned as almost one school community. Xavier boys and Mercy girls frequently traveled to school together, and because of that, over the years Sister Mary and I spent a good bit of time in the emergency room of the local hospital tending to our charges who had been in accidents on their way to or from school. On one of these occasions, Sister and I were trying to pinch hit with a girl for her parents whom we had not been able to locate. The girl was fortunately not very seriously hurt, but she was very upset and kept crying, "I want my parents. Where are my parents?" Much to my relief, her parents did arrive, and the girl calmed right down. As we were leaving the hospital, I began to reflect on how

71

different the reactions of boys and girls are in similar situations. I've spent many an hour with boys in the hospital, and in practically every instance the boy, no matter how frightened he may be, tries his damndest to put up a brave front. A frightened boy will use every ounce of his willpower to fight back tears, and although inside he may be screaming, "I want my parents," he will rarely express such a sentiment out loud. I will leave it to the experts to determine if this is inherited or learned behavior. The fact remains that boys are masters at disguising their feelings.

A senior who suddenly announces to his parents that he wants no part of college could well be indicating that he's afraid that he won't be accepted at a college or that he's having second thoughts about being sprung from the nest. "I can't wait to get out of this house and go off to college" may be the ordinary adolescent yearning for independence. It may also be the front he needs to cope with the fear he has about growing up. How many times have I seen seniors who have had a good experience at school turn sour in the last two months. If you tell yourself that you hate a place, then it's supposed to be easier to leave, isn't it? St. X has been a secure place for these young men for four years. Leaving such security is at best uncomfortable. Real men don't let people know that they're scared, do they? So up goes the "tough guy" front. "Boy I can't wait to get out of here" translates "What am I going to do when I have to leave here?"

A boy in trouble may frequently adopt an arrogant or "devil-may-care" attitude simply to cover what's really going on inside of him. Would that I had a nickel for every time that I've had to begin a conference with a boy in trouble with, "Wipe that smile off your face, junior!" He's not smiling because he's trying to be defiant. I know it, and so does he. The principal/boy dynamic is very much analogous to the father/son dynamic. The boy might be nervous as hell, but he's going to try his damnedest not to let me know that. I also wish I had a nickel for every time I've said to a boy, "It's all right to cry, you know." Tears are a lot healthier than bottled up emotions that have nowhere to go. But real men don't eat quiche, and they don't cry, do they? So the unshed tears can appear as anger or apathy or any other emotion which seems inappropriate to the situation at hand.

I remember the day my sister left home to enter the convent (which she has long since left). I was sixteen. Typical of siblings who are close in age, my sister and I had done our share of fighting, and I told everybody I was thrilled that she was going off to the convent because I was going to inherit her car, a 1960 Corvair. I smiled through the whole day despite the fact that my mother was a basket case. When we got home from leaving my sister at the convent, I decided to polish the car. One of my aunts wandered out to see what I was doing, took one look at me and said, "You miss her already, don't you?" That was all I needed. The floodgates broke, and I started to cry uncontrollably. I was amazed by my tears, but what amazed me even more was that my dad was crying. Now my mother I expected to cry, but dad? I mean men aren't supposed to do that, are they? Whether they're learned or inherited, some attitudes are most definitely handed down from generation to generation (or more particularly from father to son).

Boys are masters of disguise and masters of mixed signals. After twenty-four years of working with teenaged boys, I still can't fathom all these signals. I do know this much. Never take what a boy says or does at face value. You may not understand his actions or his emotional response in a given set of circumstances, but let me assure you, neither does he.

Over fifteen hundred years ago, Saint Benedict advised his monks, "Listen with the ear of your heart." Wise counsel! May the good Lord give us, parents and teachers, "listening hearts" to see through the adolescent disguises to the boy trying his hardest, however inappropriately at times, to become a man.

73

ON PROVIDING A UNITED FRONT

Caesar practiced it when he attacked the Gauls as did Hannibal when he marched on Italy with his elephants. It has been the strategy in every successful war since the dawn of time, and it is a principle imbedded in the heart of every adolescent boy. Divide and conquer! Be it routing the Gauls, invading Europe or convincing reluctant parents that he really should be allowed to go on the unchaperoned coed camping trip, divide and conquer works every time.

There's nothing more bothersome to the adolescent than parents who talk to each other about parenting issues and who then provide a united front when it comes to dealing with their children. Adolescents instinctively look for the chink in the armor, the slightest sign that mom and dad disagree on some "kid related" issue. Before you know it, they have mom and dad in separate rooms (they'd get them on separate planets if they could) and are attempting to divide and conquer. I'm sure that you have all experienced this more times than you would like to remember.

"It's O.K. with mom if it's O.K. with you, dad."

"I don't know why you're upset, mom. Dad said I could!"

"Before dad left on his business trip to the Himalayas where he can't possibly be reached, he told me that I could go to the dance and the party afterwards even if it does go on to 2:00 a.m. If Dad said I could go, how can you now tell me I can't."

In all these instances mom or dad probably said, "Ask your mother (or your father)," which is all the teenaged boy needs to begin his favorite strategy. Boys are always looking for the best odds, and they know just which of their parents is going to give them those odds. That's why it is so important that parents talk to each other and agree on the ground rules that are going to govern junior's life. Even if parents disagree over these ground rules, they should never let on to junior. A united front on all issues at all times is the only way to deal with a teenaged boy. He'll be furious with you for it, but in the end such a tactic will save your sanity.

Providing a united front is particularly important where there has been a divorce or a separation. I can only imagine how difficult such a situation must be, and please know that I make no judgments. It may seem that I am stating the obvious, but at a time when two adults are having serious differences with each other, it is important to remember that they can't let those differences interfere with their approach to their children. Even if mom is in Louisville and dad is in Alaska, they should agree on junior's ground rules so that he can't be making midnight calls to the Northwest looking for better odds!

The British ruled India for two centuries because the various Indian factions and religions didn't have enough unanimity to drive the British out. Hannibal and Caesar we've already discussed. You are perhaps wondering why I use military metaphors when discussing parent/son relationships. If you haven't yet experienced the "battle of wills" which is so much a part of the parent/teenager relationship, then you should be on your knees thanking God Almighty for a very singular blessing. If my military metaphor rings true to your experience, remember the united front. Provide one, and you'll save your sanity and drive your son to distraction. Far better he be driven there than you!

A LENTEN REFLECTION ON PERSPECTIVE

It's very late at night (or very early in the morning). The phone rings, and as you come slowly to consciousness, you become aware that you don't know whether your son is home or not. The lateness of the hour and the uncertainty cause a knot in your stomach and give rise to a spontaneous, anxious prayer, "Dear God, let him be all right." Perhaps the call is your son reporting a flat tire or offering some other excuse for a missed curfew, and your anxiety turns immediately into righteous parental rage. While you sputter, he stammers. That's the scenario if you're lucky. I've known far too many parents in the course of my career for whom that late night call was a summons to an emergency room or an accident scene.

       Last month when Mr. Bergamini of our faculty and his wife buried their four month old son, Father Deatrick at St. Martha's commented in his homily at the funeral that only parents who have themselves lost a child can understand what other parents are going through in that sad circumstance. Father Deatrick spoke the truth very eloquently. In my nine years as principal in Connecticut we buried nine students, and while I spent a great deal of time with the grieving parents and journeyed with them through the wake and funeral, I knew that I could never even begin to appreciate their grief. I could offer the support of my presence and the school's resources, but that support and those resources couldn't begin to touch the depth of their grief. On a number of occasions I gave the homily at the funerals of these boys who did not live to be men, and as I looked out at the parents, I knew that absolutely nothing I could say would be any consolation. Their grief was such that only time and the grace of God could begin to assuage and to heal it.

When my grandmother died in 1957, my aunt found in her effects an envelope on which my grandmother had written "to be buried with me." In the envelope was a lock of hair belonging to my father's sister Florence who died at the age of five in 1914. Over forty years later the daughter whom she had only had for five years was still in my grandmother's mind and heart, and I'm sure she would have endured anything if that daughter could have lived to adulthood. My grandmother had three other daughters and two sons, but the special place that Florence held in her heart remained until the day my grandmother died.

Theologians tell us that we should always look at life *sub specie aeternitatis,* that is, from the perspective of eternity, and I think that for the parents of a teenager, it is a perspective worth developing. On those days when your son is being absolutely impossible, on those days when you're seriously wondering why you ever decided to have children, on those days when your son's adolescence is more than you can endure, try to imagine what life would be like without him. Try to imagine how you would feel if that late night phone call weren't about a flat tire or a lame excuse. Your son's journey from boyhood to manhood is perhaps as difficult on you as it is on him, but you always need to remember that it is, hopefully, just a brief moment in what will become a very productive life. If you lost him, your grief would be beyond imagining. That's a good perspective to keep in mind on the rougher days of his adolescence.

Lent reminds us that it is impossible to live life without the shadow of the Cross, but in God's loving plan Easter and the Resurrection always triumph over the Cross. That's another good perspective to keep in mind. May the good Lord bless you and your family with happiness, peace and the joy of His Resurrection.

ON *KVELL* AND HIGH EXPECTATIONS

I was the fire drill king of all Connecticut. At the sound of the alarm, the students at Xavier High School could evacuate the building in absolute silence in less than a minute. The local fire chief adored me! On one occasion he suggested that I give instructions to the local principals on how to conduct an orderly fire drill since he was having difficulty with a few area schools which took forever to evacuate and did so in a very disorderly fashion at that. Xavier had very high expectations for fire drills, and the boys knew them. They also knew that failure to meet those high expectations would result in a three day jug. The expectations were clear, and the penalties were clear as well. As boys will do with anything, they turned the fire drills into a contest and were absolutely delighted when I informed them that they had broken a record that they had previously set. By the time I left Connecticut, they were fairly galloping out of the building when the fire bell rang.

When I came to St. Xavier, I felt it would be best not to make any significant changes in the school since the school was already top notch, but there was one minor area which I felt needed attention. I wanted the school to celebrate liturgy as an entire school community and not by individual classes as had been done in the past. On Holy Days of Obligation and on other special occasions, I wanted the entire school, faculty, staff and student body, to come together to worship. St. X had not had a good experience with student behavior at total school liturgies, and a number of teachers expressed chagrin at the thought of being in the gymnasium with the entire school. I met all objections with "We'll tell the boys what we want, and they'll do it." My experience over the years with teenaged boys is that if you set your expectations high enough and if you make those expectations very clear, they inevitably rise to the occasion. Both at Xavier in Connecticut and at St. X, I've been proud of the student body on far many more occasions than I've been disappointed. Boys *will* be boys, and common sense sometimes fails them, but on the whole they want to do the right thing, and they want to make their parents and their teachers proud of them.

I firmly believe that one of the major problems with education today is that educators and parents don't set the standards high enough for their students and children. If you expect little, you'll get little. If you expect a great deal, even more than they feel that they're capable of giving, you'll get it or a close enough approximation to make you glad that you set the standard high. Recently the principal of another high school was touring St. X with me and with Mr. Sangalli, and at the end of the tour, he was incredibly impressed by the industriousness and the deportment of the St. X student body. He asked, "How do you guys do it?" Although I didn't express it at the time, I thought to myself that for 131 years we've set the standards very high, and we've expected the students to meet those standards. For 131 years the students have been doing just that.

The expectations are high, and the expectations are clear as are the consequences of not meeting the expectations. On most school days 99% of the student body meets those expectations and even exceeds those expectations. You don't win the Blue Ribbon Award from the U.S. Department of Education three times by having a sloppy and lazy student body which settles for second best.

When we had the first Mass for the entire school last year on the Feast of All Saints, I must admit that I was a tad nervous. I had told the students very clearly what was expected, and I had assured the faculty that there would be no problem. From the altar I watched the student body like a hawk, and within the first ten minutes I had (rather visibly) ejected ten boys from the gymnasium with the instruction to go to the office and wait for me. From that point on Mass proceeded without a hitch. The thought process in the student body was almost palpable. "He said it. He meant it. We'd better do it." When I got into my first period class after that liturgy, my students were all abuzz, and one of them said, "You were just waiting, weren't you? You were determined to nab the first kid that blinked an eye." I laughed and told them that I certainly did intend to nab the first kid who "blinked an eye." I set the expectations high, and the student body had to know that I always mean what I say. After all, I was new at St. X, and they had had very little experience of me. We still have occasional lapses at school liturgies, but 99% of the student body behaves beautifully, and the liturgies have been very positive experiences.

This year at the Feast of St. Francis Xavier we concluded the liturgy with the Alma Mater. As the choir and the student body gustily sang:

> Let thy praises roar,
> Thundering to the sky,
> We will ever love thee,
> Dear St. Xavier High.

I had a Kvell moment. Kvell is a Yiddish word which means "For a parent to swell with pride and joy." That's a powerful lot of meaning for one word! My job description as given to me by the Board of Directors states that I am the spiritual leader of the school, the spiritual father if you will. On that Feast of St. Francis Xavier I experienced a tremendously joyful pride in the students and the faculty of St. X and in the Xaverian tradition of education. On May 21st when the 310 young men in the class of 1995 graduate, their parents will, indeed, "Swell with pride and joy." High expectations will give birth to high hopes as these young men go forth to make St. Xavier and their parents proud of them.

Please don't be afraid to hold your son to very high standards. Let him know clearly what you expect and make sure that he knows that you mean it. Yes, he will be relentless in trying to wear you down, as the Colorado River wore down the Rockies, but if you hold your ground, ultimately he will not disappoint you. Then your pride in the man he will become will "Thunder to the skies."

ON TALKING TURKEY ABOUT THE
SUMMER (OR IDLE MINDS
AND THE DEVIL'S WORKSHOP)

Adolescence has to be the leading cause of schizophrenia in adults. If that isn't scientific fact, it ought to be. You could develop a touch of schizophrenia just from reading my monthly newsletters. One month I tell you how important it is for your son to know deeply in his gut how profoundly you love him, and the next month I tell you to "crack the whip" and hold him responsible as you attempt to mold him into a mature man. This schizophrenic approach might be a problem for parents, but I don't think it's a problem for your sons. I have always believed quite firmly, and my experience has borne this out over twenty-four years of working with teenaged boys, that a teenaged boy wants to be held responsible. He wants to know what's expected of him, and he understands quite clearly, although he'll never admit it, that "tough love" is still love.

With that as a background, let me give you a few helpful hints about surviving the summer. I warn you that you will be as popular with your son for heeding these hints as I will be for giving them to you,

Idle Minds And The Devil's Workshop: Not long ago as I was winging my way on USAir from Baltimore to Louisville, I sat next to a young widow who had two sons ages 11 and 12 1/2. Our conversation, which lasted for the entire flight, deserves its own letter, and it will probably get that next year. Her husband had died suddenly when the older of the two boys was six, and she had been left to cope on her own. Unfortunately, she had no brothers, and all of her friends had produced girls, so she was left to figure boys out on her own. Once I had assured her that the intense sibling rivalry that she was experiencing in her sons was perfectly normal, she gave me her recipe for coping with her situation. "I keep them so busy they don't have time to give me any trouble. I sign them up for anything they can be signed up for: Little League, basketball camp, soccer camp, tennis lessons, Boy Scouts, Cub Scouts, swimming lessons, anything I can find. Of course, I spend my life in a car driving them hither and yon, but it's worth it. Apart from their school work, I don't give them time to think." I applauded her wisdom because her insight into the nature of the adolescent (and pre-adolescent) male exactly coincides with my own. The more a teenaged boy has to do, the less chance he has to get into trouble. If he's old enough to get a job this summer, make sure he gets one. God knows that you could use some help paying his tuition and fees at St. X. If he's not old enough to work or he can't find a job, sign him up for anything you can sign him up for or encourage him to do volunteer work. A teenager with nothing to do in the summer is a teenager whose mind is open to becoming "the devil's workshop."

Where? With Whom? How Long? These are questions to be asked whenever your son leaves the house. If he responds, "Riding around with the guys," you have a higher probability of hearing from the police by the end of the night than you would if he responds, "With Joe and Jeff to Mary's house to listen to music." Get to know your son's friends, and if possible, get to know his friends' parents. Known quantities are always better than unknown quantities.

Curfew? None Of My Friends Have Curfews! I have been truly amazed in recent years to discover that many parents don't set curfews for their sons. Of course he shouldn't have to be in before dark, and yes, because he goes to a high school which draws students from all of Louisville and the surrounding counties, his friends may live in Bullitt County while he lives in St. Matthews. No matter where his friends live, 3 AM is a tad late for a high school boy to be out. Bad things happen in the middle of the night. Believe me, I've answered too many early morning phone calls, and I know the potential here for trouble. Set a curfew. Make it reasonable, but set one, and enforce it.

If I'm Old Enough To Work, I'm Old Enough To Handle My Own Money! Definitely not. If he has a bank account and a steady job, you should be monitoring his cash flow. Parents who don't do this run the risk of discovering that there is nothing in their son's bank account at the same time that the police or the principal is telling them that their son has a substance abuse problem. In September I wrote you about my concerns with alcohol and substance abuse among St. X students. You'll be sad to know that cocaine has appeared in the Louisville high school scene, and if it has appeared in the Louisville high school scene, it has probably appeared at St. X. Monitor your son's cash flow! Believe me when I tell you that I know what I'm talking about here.

No, You Can't Have A Few Friends In While we're Away. If you leave your son alone at home for a few days, I'd have Aunt Martha or Grandpa or Uncle Pete make a number of unannounced house checks. I'll never forget the day an enraged father arrived in my office wanting to kill his son and his cohorts for destroying the man's home at a party which had gotten out of hand while he and his wife were enjoying a well-deserved romantic weekend in the country. That's just one example. I could go on.

Sex, Drugs, And Rock And Roll: Summer is a good time for dad to have a man-to-man (or man-to-boy becoming man) talk about sex, alcohol, drugs and the good life. Be brief. Be blunt. Boys don't understand subtlety. Be specific. You've probably noticed that your son is an aspiring attorney always looking for the loopholes. Will he listen? Maybe not, but it's worth a try.

Pray! This summer, whenever your son goes out, ask the important questions, insist on specific, verifiable answers and then pray. Abraham Lincoln once said, "I have often been driven to my knees by the overwhelming conviction that I had nowhere else to go." As he grows older, there are so many things in your son's life over which you will have little control. Resign yourself to this fact as best you can and then remind God frequently that watching over your son is His job.

All of the above having been said, let me tell you how happy I am that you have him for the summer. I'll be praying for you. Enjoy!

ON IVAN THE TERRIBLE AND HOW I FIRST LEARNED ABOUT THE NATURE OF THE BEAST

The kids called him "Ivan the Terrible" and a few other choice epithets which related to his girth. He weighed in at about 300 pounds, and he stood a lowering 5'4". The Brothers always affectionately referred to him as "Big Daddy." Brother Ivan had been a superior and principal for a good part of his fifty years of religious life when I had the good fortune to have him as the superior on my first mission. Common sense was his strong suit. A master teacher and a very kind man, Brother Ivan was a fine example for a young Brother trying to "learn the trade."

Brother Ivan and I taught next to each other during my first year in the classroom. We were in the lower school building at St. John's High, and midway through the morning all of the students in the lower building returned to the main building and were replaced by students who had spent the first few periods in the main building. The whole process took about six minutes, and during that time I would wander into Brother Ivan's classroom. Since his size didn't lend itself to much movement, Brother Ivan rarely left his desk. I would sit down in one of the student desks, and Brother Ivan would give me pointers on how to become a school teacher. It was in these brief daily sessions with Brother Ivan that I first began to learn about "the nature of the beast."

Brother Ivan had a few assumptions about teen-aged boys and their education. Boys are not natural students At least Ivan had run into very few in fifty years who were. Boys can find 10,000 things that they would rather do than study, and, that being the case, the good teacher was certainly silly to get overly upset when boys didn't study. In fact, practically each of our daily conferences would begin with "Jimmy, you shouldn't yell so much. They're not going to study any harder because you yell." He was strong on memorization. "They'll never learn to think clearly if they don't have their facts straight." The good teacher was the one who could find 350 ways to explain the same thing, and when that didn't work, could come up with a 351st. And drill! Brother Ivan was a firm believer in the "pound it into their heads" philosophy of education. He also firmly believed that the more grades you had, the better chance the boys had of getting good grades. Brother Ivan's grade book went on for pages, and daily quizzes were the norm. Perhaps the greatest lesson I learned from him came every night as I would watch this 67-year-old man correcting papers in the Brothers' common room.

Brother Ivan understood that boys tend to whine a bit when they are worked hard, and he also knew that they frequently don't or can't articulate what they really feel. With the insecurity of the first year teacher, I mentioned on a couple of occasions to him that I didn't think my students liked me. His response was immediate and quite clear. "It's not important whether or not the boys like you. It is important that they respect you, and they'll respect you if you're fair with them, work them hard and teach them well. They'll complain like the dickens when you work them, but boys know instinctively when they've been well taught. That's your job to teach them well. If you do that, they'll respect you, and they'll probably end up liking you." That bit of advice has served me well over twenty-five years, and as a school administrator, I've given it to many a first-year teacher. If you change teaching to parenting, there's certainly a lesson in Brother Ivan's words for parents who are on their first voyage through a son's adolescence.

Brother Ivan was the consummate realist. He never expected boys not to the boys. Not that he took any nonsense from them. He could be like a Panzer tank when dealing with unruly behavior, and the boys had a healthy fear of provoking him. He accepted boys for what they are, and he knew that, in God's good time, they would become men. The rule of the Xaverian Brothers which was in effect for most of Brother Ivan's religious life advised the Brothers always "to respect the man the boy will become." Brother Ivan understood boys perfectly, and he understood perfectly how hard they have to struggle to become men. Watching generations of school boys become mature, productive men had given him incredible faith in the power of God's grace at work in the maturing process.

At Christmas time in 1978, Brother Ivan died peacefully after over fifty years in the religious life and in the classroom. He had retired from teaching only six months before his death, and many of the Brothers thought that his timing was perfect. It was hard for any of us to imagine Ivan out of the classroom and in retirement. To this day when I picture him in my memory, I see a man in his late sixties wearing his religious habit, his black topcoat and a black soft hat with a whistle around his neck prefecting forty freshmen in an after school game of street hockey on a chilly November day. When I was a young Brother in the Novitiate, we were taught that one of the hallmarks of a Xaverian Brother is zeal for the welfare of the young men in his charge. Brother Ivan's daily life was an unspoken lesson to all of the young Brothers in the community on what it means to be zealous.

Brother Ivan is certainly one of the "saints" whom God has sent into my life, and as I have grown older, I have come to understand what he saw so clearly. Boys become men, Some do this sooner, others later, but become men they do. When you and I get discouraged because the process seems to be taking longer than we'd like, then we should remember Brother Ivan who never let himself become discouraged by "the nature of the beast."

May the good Lord bless you and your families with happiness and peace, and may He bless the entire St. X community as we begin the 132nd year.

ON SISTER ANNA CATHERINE
AND SHORT CIRCUITING PETER PAN

She couldn't have been five feet tall. Even at the age of 14, I towered over her, and God knows that there aren't many people over whom I tower. Short as she was, she managed daily to terrorize 150 or so adolescent boys and girls. I remember one boy in my class, a football player no less, who adamantly refused to come to school on Wednesday afternoons because she presided over a double period of Latin drill on that day. The thought of her "call cards" and her withering stare were apparently too much for him. You never ever thought of offering her an excuse even if you had a perfectly good one. She didn't take excuses. When I managed to fail Latin and religion during the first marking period of my freshman year, she called my father. I couldn't hear her, of course, but my father's side of the conversation was quite simple. "Yes, Sister. Yes, Sister. No, Sister. I'm sorry, Sister. I'll speak with him, Sister. I'm sorry, Sister. Thank you, Sister." My dad was the administrator of a large hospital, and he was not used to apologizing to anybody. I knew then that if he were apologizing for my existence, my existence wasn't going to be worth much for a good time to come. It wasn't. I never failed anything else in twenty-one more years of schooling!

"School boy" and "excuse" are about as synonymous as two words can get. On rare occasions the excuses are good and valid. Most of the time they are nothing more than a cover for laziness or irresponsibility or both. Kids and their excuses never discourage me. I expect them. I probably would be disappointed if they didn't at least make the attempt. What does discourage me, and mightily at that, is the increasing number of parents who make excuses for their sons, parents who are quite ready to blame everyone but their son for his failures. I'm sorry if that sounds harsh, and I realize that I have the comfortable perspective of a celibate who doesn't have the difficult task of raising children. I do, however, have the advantage of never escaping adolescence (not my own hopefully), and after twenty-five years of slugging it out with the youth of America, I can guarantee you that a boy will never learn responsibility until he has had to face the full brunt of the consequences of irresponsibility. Make a habit of bailing him out now, and he will be looking for someone to bail him out when he's forty.

For better or for worse, in all of us men there is a bit of Peter Pan, the boy who refused to grow up. A boy cannot learn too early in his adolescence that Peter Pan has to be discouraged rather than encouraged. Some life lessons are better and more easily learned at sixteen. Once I discovered that my winning smile and Irish charm were going to cut no mustard with Sister Anna Catherine and once I realized that my Dad was backing the nun and not his only son, I buckled down and went to work. Despite our bumpy beginning, Sister Anna Catherine and I went on to become great friends, and she was fond of telling the story of the fourteen year old whom she had failed in Latin and religion who went on to become a religious with a degree in Latin and Greek.

When I was fourteen, however, 149 other freshmen and I disliked Sister Anna Catherine intensely. The boys disliked her particularly because she was a mortal enemy of Peter Pan and had absolutely no respect for our burgeoning male egos. At fourteen I disliked her. At forty-eight I bless the day she came into my life.

A bit of Peter Pan can be refreshing. If Peter gets the upper hand, however, your son's life could end up in "Never Never Land." Some life lessons are far more easily and less painfully learned when you're sixteen. Protect your son from whatever in this world might really harm him, but please don't protect him from growing up.

ON WISE WIDOWS AND CONVERSATIONS
AT 33,000 FEET

She looked so absolutely terrified that I became seriously concerned. Since I spend an inordinate amount of time on USAir as I wing my way back and forth between Louisville and Boston or Baltimore, flying has become just part of the day, and I use the time in the air either to sleep or to work and rarely to engage my fellow passengers in conversation since one horrible flight from Boston to Pittsburgh when the man next to me insisted on giving me the details of his rather bizarre sex life. This poor woman, however, was obviously not an experienced flyer and in such sad straits that I began a conversation to get her mind off her terror. We had both been upgraded to first class, and she had a double scotch before we took off. The scotch and her terror made her quite ready to talk. She was a young widow whose husband had died when her older son was six, and now five years after her husband's death, she was on her way to Louisville to meet the family of the man whom she had been dating very seriously for the past year. The thought of meeting a possible new mother-in-law might also have added to her terror!

When she discovered that I was the head of a boys' high school, she began to talk about her two boys who were 10 1/2 and 12 years old. She decided that I could give her some professional input since, as she said, "I have no brothers, and all of my friends have produced girls. I have no one to tell me what's normal for boys and what isn't." Her first question was about sibling rivalry, and I asked if her sons had had an actual fist fight yet. She looked at me in horror. "Will that happen?" With two boys who are only eighteen months apart in age, I suggested that it was one likely scenario, but I tried to assure her that intense sibling rivalry was fairly normal behavior which she would probably have to endure through their adolescent years. "They're so competitive with each other," she said, "And at times it frightens me because their rivalry seems to be so intense. The younger one is actually physically stronger than the older one and more athletic. That bothers the older one incredibly, and the younger one certainly presses the advantage whenever he can." At that I just laughed thinking of the number of brothers I've experienced over the years who have exhibited the same behaviors. Most parents could readily assert that sibling rivalry is not the figment of some psychologist's imagination.

After I had assured her that she was seeing nothing abnormal in her sons' behavior, I asked how they felt about her boyfriend. Again she looked terrified and asked what I meant. I explained that boys can be very protective of their mothers and that I would be surprised if her boys didn't have strong opinions about this new man in her life. "They like him, and he likes them. I don't think I'd be going to meet his parents if there was a real tension between the boys and my boyfriend. I dated one man a few years ago whom they absolutely loathed, and I just knew that the whole thing wouldn't work." I was amazed by this woman's very sound instincts, and again I thought of a number of times over the years when I've seen teenaged boys be very protective of their mothers. Sometimes a teenaged boy's feelings about his mother's boyfriend or new husband can be seriously clouded by his own loyalty to his father, but I've been amazed at the number of times when the boy's instincts seem to be right on target.

This wise widow instinctively followed almost perfectly all of Kelly's principles on coping with boys. Her sons were involved in every conceivable sport and activity. She kept them as busy as she possibly could so that they were too busy to get themselves into trouble. She got to know her sons' friends and their friends' parents. She always knew where her boys were and with whom they were. Her approach to parenting exhibited incredible common sense, but apparently her friends didn't have the same perceptions. "Some of my friends feel that I'm too strict with my boys, but I'm all by myself. I can't afford to lose control of them." I've seen too many teenagers out of control not to have a healthy respect for a parent who recognizes the need to keep a teenage boy on a tight leash, and I applauded her wisdom.

Landing in Louisville brought with it a whole new set of noises and terrors, and as I talked her through that trauma, I couldn't help thinking that her two sons were very fortunate indeed to have such a mother and that the boyfriend, if he had any sense at all, would get this lady to the altar as quickly as possible. At the end of the flight I was very happy that I had violated my rule about no conversations at 33,000 feet, and as I drove back to St. X, I thought that my wise widow could certainly come to life again in one of my newsletters. And so she has!

May the good Lord bless her, and may He bless us with wise hearts as we travel with the young men in our lives on their journey to adulthood.

97

ON THE SEASONS OF ADOLESCENCE AND
THE SEASON OF ADVENT

Billy had had an extremely difficult sophomore year, and well into his junior year his problems showed no sign of abating. Since I was the disciplinarian of the school during those two years, I breathed a sigh of relief and offered a grateful prayer when in the second semester of his junior year Billy began at last to show signs of growing up.

At the beginning of his senior year, I became the Principal of the school, and wanting to keep a watchful eye on him, I had Billy assigned to my senior English class. Billy was not thrilled! As the year progressed, however, Billy and I began to develop an appreciation for each other. One afternoon after school Billy and I were working on some of his grammatical difficulties when he looked at me somewhat bemusedly and asked, "When did you become such a nice guy?" Not at all nonplussed, I laughed and replied, "About the same time that you ceased being a surly know-it-all." My reply struck Billy as extremely funny. "You must have been talking to my dad. He told me the other day that he was actually beginning to like me again. I guess I made everybody's life pretty difficult, but, for the life of me, I don't know why. I was just miserable, and I wanted everyone else to suffer with me."

My friend Billy had suffered from a very severe "sophomore season" on his journey through high school. I call it "sophomore season" because it normally hovers around the sophomore year although it can begin in the middle of freshman year and can extend (in a severe case) through the junior year. You'll know that your son is in this season if, like Billy's father, you find that, although you love him dearly, you don't much like your son. It is the season of high puberty, raging hormones and a growing sense of independence which is frustrated by the fact that he's only fifteen and has little opportunity to exercise his independence. It is very much an "in-between" season. He's not a freshman at the bottom of the heap, but he's not really an upperclassman. The tug of puberty tells him that he's no longer a boy, but he's not yet a man. He's confused, and the confusion makes him angry, and inappropriately, he directs that anger at the people who are most important to him. Unconsciously and unintentionally a boy in the sophomore season of his adolescence says without words to the adults in his life "I defy you to love me."

The "seasons of adolescence" can be very troubling to the adults in the adolescent's life, and while it may not make these seasons easier to bear, adults can take some comfort in the fact that these seasons are as puzzling to the adolescent as they are to the people who love him.

Miserable as he is himself and miserable as he might make you, he does need to know that you do still love him even if you don't particularly like him at this point in his life.

That does not mean, however, that you have to tolerate any unacceptable behavior which may accompany this season. One of my favorite lines with sophomores is "Your father may have to tolerate that tone of voice from you, young man, but I'm not your father, and I don't!" It's a great line, but it's not really true. Neither his father nor his mother have to tolerate the argumentative surliness that accompany this season of adolescence. You may not tolerate it, but it is, nonetheless, very wearing.

The sophomore season of an adolescent's life usually ends as quickly as it began, and there is no cure. Once it begins, it has to run its course, and the adults in the adolescent's life need a great deal of patience. In the nine years that I was a Principal, I probably expelled more sophomores than I did boys in any other grade level. I probably could have trebled the number of expulsions, but, whenever I could, I tried to understand. Unfortunately, boys who are in a rather severe sophomore season of life can back an adult into some pretty difficult corners.

We have just begun the beautiful season of Advent when the Church waits with patient longing for the coming of Christ at Christmas. In the second reading of the Third Sunday of Advent, St. James admonishes us:

> *Be patient until the coming of the Lord. See how the farmer awaits the precious yield of the soil. He looks forward to it patiently while the soil receives the winter and the spring rains. You too must be patient. Steady your hearts because the coming of the Lord is at hand.* (James 5:7-10)

As the Church waits patiently for the coming of the Lord at Christmas, so you too must wait patiently for your son to make that difficult transition from boy to man. As surely as Christ will come at Christmas, your son will become a man, and as the Church rejoices at Christmas, so you will rejoice to see the man he will become. But for now it takes patient endurance. The sophomore season of adolescence, like all seasons, will pass!

ON FATHERS AND SONS

"I get a shock every time I think of George setting out to be a family man. That great gangling thing. I tell you there's nothing so terrifying in the world as a son. The relationship between a father and a son is the damndest, awkwardest . . ."
—From *Our Town* by Thornton Wilder

Joe was in serious difficulty, and I had called home to summon his father to discuss the problems the school was having with him. Joe's mother answered the phone and begged, "Please, Brother, let me come and handle this. Joey and his father are not getting along very well right now, and I'd be very grateful if you'd keep this whole matter between you and me." Of course I agreed, and within minutes Joe's mother arrived with her mother-in-law in tow for moral support. When I began to re-count Joe's crimes and misdemeanors, his grandmother laughed and said, "I remember being called twenty-five years ago into a Brother's office to hear almost exactly the same story about Joey's father. My, my, the apple hasn't fallen far from the tree!" With that his mother added, "That's the problem, Brother. They're just too much alike, and it's driving me crazy."

Bicker and fight with his mother though he may, a boy (and I suppose a man as well) knows instinctively that there is nothing he can do, no matter how awful, that will make her stop loving him. He doesn't need to win her love. He has it simply because he's her child. Unfortunately a boy does not always have the same instinctive feeling about his father. In the boy's world view, his father's love has to be won. There are tests, real or imagined, that he has to pass if he is going to gain his father's love and respect. This is sad because, while he can depend on his mother's love, a boy needs his father's love and approval more than anything whether he will admit that fact or not.

Thornton Wilder hit the nail on the head when he said that the relationship between a father and a son is the "damndest, awkwardest" relationship there is. I suspect that most men spend a good part of their life attempting to win their father's approval. The difficulties in a father-son relationship might be most obvious during the son's adolescent years when he is living at home, but the relationship can remain tricky throughout life. Some fathers and sons develop a beautiful and easygoing relationship between them, but in my experience, these cases are rather rare. I can't tell you how many times I've heard a father tell me that he's envious of the relationship that his father has with his son. The grandfather-grandson relationship can be much more easygoing because the grandfather doesn't feel responsible for his grandson in the same way that, as a father, he felt responsible for his son. I know that sounds vague, but I think there's some real truth there. Perhaps in this modern world grandpa has more time to spend with his grandson than the boy's father does. Unfortunately, there's also some real truth to the Harry Chapin song *The Cat's in the Cradle* about the father who didn't have time for his son when the boy was growing up. When the father finally realizes his mistake, his son doesn't have any time for him.

Fathers want their sons to grow up to be men who can handle themselves in a rough and cruel world, and at times, I think, they are afraid that if they are too soft with their sons while they are young, the sons will not be capable of handling themselves in the "man's" world they will have to face. Perhaps, as Joe's mother suggested, fathers are hard on sons because they see too much of themselves in their sons. Perhaps sons are difficult because they have similar perceptions. Whatever the case may be, as long as there are fathers and sons living in one house, there are going to be conflicts.

Can you resolve these conflicts? I wish I had a pat answer that would bring father and son together, but I don't. I do think that since the father is the adult in the situation, he is probably the one who is going to have to work hardest to resolve whatever conflicts he and his son might have. I go back to my original premise. Whether he admits it or not, a boy wants his father's love and approval more than anything in this world. The love and the approval are certainly there, but if the boy does not perceive the situation accurately, then it's up to dad to correct this faulty perception. We will celebrate soon the feast of the Baptism of Jesus. St. Luke tells us that when Jesus was baptized, God the Father's voice was heard saying, "You are my beloved son. In you I am well pleased." As with God the Father and Jesus, so with you and your son. Make sure, Dad, that your son knows that when it comes to him, you and God feel the same way.

ON SIBLING RIVALRY

Lest you think that I have gone senile, I do realize that I touched upon sibling rivalry in my November letter on the wise widow, but since at St. X alone we have seventy-six sets of brothers, I suspect that most St. X parents have a good bit of experience with sibling rivalry. That being the case, I'd like to offer a few reflections on sibling rivalry, and, of course, my reflections will require a story or two.

Scott had been in a fight and had landed in my office to give an account of himself. When I asked why he had "clocked" one of his classmates, he replied, "Because he was picking on my brother." Now I knew that Scott and his younger brother barely tolerated each other and would probably be in different schools if Scott had anything to say about it. I pointed this out to Scott. Looking at me as if I were dim-witted, he stated as a self-evident truth, "I can pick on my brother, but nobody else can."

In one of his Epistles St. Paul asks, "Who can fathom the mind of God?" There are times when I think it would be far easier to fathom the mind of God than to fathom the mind of an adolescent boy. As my conversation with Scott continued, I discovered that he had a bedrock loyalty to his kid brother. Perhaps this loyalty was apparent to his brother. I actually think it was. It was not at all apparent to his parents or to anyone else who watched these two young men together.

The closer two siblings are in age, the more intense the rivalry between them will be. Any parent in this situation can attest to the fact that sibling rivalry is not the figment of some psychologist's imagination. The naturally competitive nature that is so much a part of a boy seems to increase dramatically when it involves a sibling, be that sibling a brother or a sister. Perhaps your children are in a contest for mom's or dad's attention or for pecking order in the household. Most likely they are trying to prove something to themselves more than to anyone else.

Sounds pretty vague, doesn't it? I don't know the reasons, and I don't think there's a cure. I just know that sibling rivalry is a fact of life. As I mentioned above, we have seventy-six boys at St. X who have a brother in school. Over the course of the school year I watch many of these brothers make a point of ignoring each other. I've seen countless boys blossom when their older brothers graduate. They return to school in August almost as new persons and rededicate themselves to the task of proving to their teachers, their classmates and themselves that they are not just some other guy's brother.

No parent or school teacher deliberately compares siblings in the presence of one of them, but sometimes, human beings that we are, we accidentally make a comparison. Early on in my career I called a boy by his older brother's name. An easy mistake. Teaching both boys as I did, I had the last name in my head and the wrong first name to go along with it. Unfortunately the older brother was one of those young men who seemed to have it all—intelligent, good looking and athletic. In fact his teachers had dubbed him, somewhat tongue in cheek, "Boy wonder." The younger brother, by far the more likeable of the two, did not find life the piece of cake that his brother seemed to find it. I called him by his brother's name. He burst into tears and ran out of the classroom. Unaware of my blunder, I was puzzled by his action. The class, however, was not. My mistake was quite evident to them. Almost in a chorus they said, "Brother, no kid wants to be called by his brother's name. " I found Chris and apologized, but I was young then and wondered why this boy was making such a fuss over a minor mistake. As I've grown older, I've come to realize just what a serious matter it is to a fifteen-year-old that his teachers (and his parents) know who he is and appreciate him for his uniqueness. And how important it is that he not be confused with his brother!!

The best we as parents and school teachers can do is to remind ourselves constantly that brothers (and sisters) can be as different as night and day and that they have to be treated as such. Each one has to know that he (or she) is unique and special in our eyes. We probably won't find a cure for sibling rivalry, and we will never fully understand it. I know of at least one mother with three sons very close in age who periodically threatened to leave home if they didn't stop fighting with each other. Patience is the key here. They'll grow up sooner than you think and leave home. Then when the house is just too quiet, you'll probably long for the days when battling siblings made the house just too noisy.

Isn't it a good thing that you didn't know how complicated raising children was going to be when you first decided to have them? May the good Lord bless you with patience, energy and the stamina necessary to survive your son's adolescence.

ON THE ADOLESCENT BOY AND HIS JOB
(Or Why He'd Rather Work at McDonald's
Than Do His Homework)

When I was a boy in high school, many of my friends and I
worked in a local Jewish delicatessen and restaurant. The owner
of this bistro, Harry, insisted on hiring as many students from
the Catholic high school as he could. "These Catholic school
kids are always responsible, and they work hard," Harry was
wont to comment to anyone who would listen. He also liked
the fact that we Catholic school students were neat since we
came right from school in the standard early 1960's Catholic
school attire, the girls in shapeless blue jumpers, white blouses
and blue bows and the boys in sports jackets, ties and dress
pants loose enough so that a golf ball could drop down them
without any trouble.

The attire may have changed since then, but the reality hasn't. St. Xavier students have always been and continue

to be a significant segment in the local adolescent work force, and I'm sure that their industry and responsibility have earned them the respect of their employers. On one Saturday morning last August, I walked into the Winn-Dixie on Breckinridge Lane to be greeted with a chorus of "Hi, Brother" from eight St. X students who were working as cashiers or baggers in the front of the store. On that Saturday morning it appeared as if St. X had the Winn-Dixie well under control! There is, however, one minor hitch to this adolescent enthusiasm for work. Boys, unfortunately, love to work a lot more than they love to do school work.

The formula is quite simple: Work equals money equals independence. There is a variation on the formula: Work equals increased self-esteem equals money equals independence. The constants are money and independence, but the bottom line is independence.

Many, if not all, of the conflicts which you will have with your son as he grows older will center on his perception that he is a man and that he has a right to call the shots in his life. "It's my life!" How many times have you heard that one? An integral part of the growth of a boy to manhood is an increasing desire for control over his own life and destiny. The problem is that the "boy-not-quite-yet-a-man" does not have the experience and the wisdom of age, and with his newly emerging freedom, he often doesn't make the wisest of choices.

A boy loves to work because it gives him a sense of freedom and independence. He's earning money on his own. Isn't that a sign that he's grown up? His boss at Burger King or Winn-Dixie or Kroger's trusts him and likes his work. The boss doesn't nag him like his parents and teachers tend to do. In school he doesn't see very many concrete signs that his effort is paying off, but at work there is the weekly paycheck and perhaps the pat on the back from a grateful employer. In school he may be doing well, but stacking shelves or bagging groceries is a lot easier and far more "hands on" than Algebra

II or English Literature.

Thus, the problem. A boy would usually far prefer to make his job his first priority and his school work a distant second priority. He'll get as many hours as he can at work, and if that means his homework is done poorly or not done at all, so be it. The attitude is incredibly adolescent and thus incredibly shortsighted. Enter farsighted mom and dad to put the brakes on junior's ride in the world of work. I have no rule of thumb here, but if your son is working twenty hours or more a week, he's probably working too much. Now if most of these hours are on the weekend, perhaps he can swing it, but a weekend that is all work and no play does not leave him in a very good frame of mind to begin school on Monday.

Please monitor your son's work life and make sure that he has his priorities straight: School first. Always keep in mind *Kelly's Rule of Thumb on Cash Flow.* Bank accounts should be joint with mom and dad, and mom and dad should monitor the account to make sure the money is there. If it isn't, mom and dad should know where it went.

Do you remember *Snow White and the Seven Dwarfs?* The dwarfs used to sing, "Hi-ho, hi-ho, it's off to work we go!" You and I haven't sung that in years. Your son sings it everyday with joy in his heart as he heads to Kroger's or the Winn Dixie. He doesn't realize yet that he has the rest of his life to work and that we adults, for all our independence, long to have the "freedom" of adolescence. With time he will probably come to our rather jaded adult perspective. Our job now is to see that when he gets to that point, he arrives there with a good, solid education on which he can build.

Getting a shortsighted adolescent to think like a farsighted adult is something akin to transporting the Mojave Desert to Bangor, Maine, in a pickup truck. Good luck! May the good Lord bless you with the necessary patience and fortitude.

ON NOT MAKING THE CUT

On an unusually balmy February afternoon, as I left school, I came upon a young man who looked rather upset. When I asked him if he were all right, he said much too quickly and with an obvious show of bravado, "I'm fine. I'm just fine." As I walked out to my car, I began to wonder what was troubling the lad, and then it dawned on me. Brother Robert Flaherty had told me just the day before that he was going to make the first round of cuts from the freshman baseball team, and I had just come upon one of the boys who didn't make the cut. This young man didn't need to give up anything for Lent. Life had just provided him with his Lenten penance.

Unfortunately, not making the cut, whether it be for a team, for the school play or for a college, is part of adolescent life. In the panorama of life, not making the freshman baseball team is a minor disappointment unless, of course, you are a freshman in high school.

Teenaged boys live very much for the moment, and at the moment that they are cut from a team or refused by a college, all they feel is the pain of rejection, and it seems to them that pain will continue forever. My first inclination, after I realized that the young man had been cut from the team, was to go back and to talk with him, but I learned long ago that in the heat of the moment nothing I could say would ease the boy's pain. He had to live with it for a while, and perhaps then an adult could help him to put it into perspective, but not immediately, not while the wound was still so raw.

Getting cut from a team or refused by a college is as difficult for his parents as it is for the young man involved. Parents, of course, never want to see their son in pain, and they are confronted simultaneously with their son's pain and with their inability to do anything about it. There is the added realization that perhaps there really are other young men who are more talented athletically or more gifted academically than their son. Parents might accept that fact on an intellectual level, but when they are confronted with a son in pain, the realization becomes rather stark and perhaps more real than an intellectual concept. I hope that you will forgive me if I become rather blunt, but it is my sad experience that very frequently parents, when confronted with these realizations, tend to assign blame not to their son's abilities but to the coaches or colleges making the decision about their son's abilities. You and I both know that there are far too many adults in the world who blame their failures on everyone but themselves. Please do not teach your son to grow into one of those adults.

It is an unfortunate fact of life that you as parents will not be able to protect your son from the "slings and arrows of outrageous fortune" as Shakespeare put it. He is going to have to learn to deal with disappointment and with rejection in his life if he is to grow into a mature man. You and I know that being cut from a team or being rejected by a college or being "dumped" by your first girlfriend is not the end of the world. Your son doesn't know that. When his pain begins to subside, your job as parents is to help him put his experience into perspective and accept the limitations which life may impose on him. That task becomes all the more difficult since you have to help him accept limitations at the same time that you encourage him to try again and to push himself to his limits and perhaps beyond.

There is an old, rather pious but very truthful adage that God never closes a door unless He opens a window. Two years ago, one St. X student who was cut from baseball became an integral part of our record setting 400 meter relay team in track. An alumnus whom I met recently in Texas told me the story of how he was cut in his junior year from our football team in the days when we dressed only fifty-five players and how he went on to make the team in his senior year and to score the winning touchdown in the opening game of the season. Last January there was an article in *The Courier Journal* about Drew Cooper who graduated from St. X last June. Drew had been cut from our basketball team repeatedly, but he did not give up his aspirations to play basketball in college. He is now playing for Assumption College in Worcester, Massachusetts (my hometown!), and is doing very well. These are just a few examples, but every year boys who have been cut from soccer or baseball or basketball find the open window and new interests.

When your son experiences the unavoidable vicissitudes of life, you are obviously going to feel his pain, and you are going to give him your emotional support. If he is to grow from the experience, however, emotional support is not enough. Your job is to help him gain a new perspective and discover new possibilities in the rubble of shattered dreams. Your job is to help him find the window that God opened when He closed the door.

You will receive this letter as Holy Week begins, and although this letter might not seem appropriate to this sacred season, I believe that it is. You cannot always protect your son from the Good Fridays of life, but you can help him to find the wonderfully new perspective of Easter. As we celebrate this Holy Week, may the good Lord help you to do just that.

ON YOUR SON'S (ETERNAL) HAPPINESS

Q. Why did God make me?
A. God made me to know Him, to love Him, to serve Him in this world and to be happy with Him forever in the next.

—The Baltimore Catechism

In the recesses of every adult mind, there is the memory of a parent saying, "Someday you'll thank me." Those words, "Someday you'll thank me," sum up beautifully and, at times, painfully the parental dilemma. As parents, you know that so frequently what your son wants is not what he needs. Your son wants happiness now, in the short run, while you are concerned about his happiness in the long run. So you act as you know you must, and you try to make him understand by saying, "Someday you'll thank me." He doesn't buy it just as you didn't buy it so many years ago.

115

The Baltimore Catechism is long out of vogue in Catholic circles, but, dogmatic and dry as its theology was, its questions and answers contained a great deal of practical wisdom. God has never promised us happiness in the short run. If He had, then He certainly shortchanged His own son. The Gospels mention that Jesus spent much of His time in prayer, talking with His Father, struggling with the painful nature of His mission. Do you think that perhaps God the Father replied, "Look, I know this is tough, but in the long run you'll thank me"? I suspect He did. In obeying His Father, Jesus won for us happiness in the long run, eternal happiness. Unfortunately there are no guarantees that between now and eternity we are going to find happiness in the short run.

Your son has been brought up in a society that worships instant gratification. The media would have him believe that happiness is as simple as the right deodorant or a new sports car. You and I know how silly that is, but your son hasn't lived long enough to learn this sobering lesson. He wants happiness now, and he can make your life rather unpleasant when he doesn't get it. When you know that what he wants is not what he needs, you hold out and repeat your own parents' words, "Someday you'll thank me."

A few years ago when I was the Principal at Xavier in Connecticut, a young man who had transferred out of the school in the middle of his junior year returned to visit. When Patrick was a student at Xavier, I harangued him frequently about his attitude, the company he was keeping and the way he was treating his parents. He, of course, took the position that I was "busting his chops" and making his life miserable. On his visit he gave me a rather honest update of his life, and, like a broken record, I launched into my harangue. After fifteen minutes he got up, smiled and said, "Thank you, Brother." I was a bit nonplused and asked, "Thanks for what?" He replied, "I knew what you'd say when you heard my story, and I also knew that

I needed to hear it. That's why I came today, to hear you tell me what I needed to hear. I finally realized you were always on my case because you cared about me. Where I'm in school now they don't really care what happens to me." With that he left. Perhaps I needed to hear the "Thanks" as much as he needed to hear the lecture. Patrick thought that leaving a Catholic school with all its rules and regulations was going to make him happy. Apparently it hadn't.

Coping with an adolescent who is not getting his way is one of life's more unpleasant experiences as I'm sure you have already discovered. The fact remains that very frequently what a teenaged boy wants is definitely not what he needs. By his very nature as an adolescent male, your son does not think of the long-term consequences. As his parents you have to do that for him. When you think back to your own parents, the "someday" of "someday you'll thank me" is now, and although you may never have expressed it, you are grateful. Trust that someday your own children will thank you for being concerned with their happiness in the long run rather than in the short. I'm afraid you'll have to wait for the grandchildren before you can start fulfilling their every desire without worrying about the consequences. Then, in a wonderful turning of the tables, you can leave your son to deal with consequences!

ON REDISCOVERING OLD INSIGHTS

The more I know, the less I understand
All the things I thought I knew, I'm learning again
—From the Song *Forgiveness* by Don Henley

I have come to the conclusion after forty-nine years of life that much of life consists of remembering things that you have already learned and rediscovering insights which you have already had. Every month I write to you about the insights I have had over twenty-five years of working with teenaged boys in the hope that my insights might help make the process of parenting a teenager a bit easier for you. If at times I seem to become repetitive, please don't think that I repeat myself because I think that you are dimwitted. I repeat myself because, at times, I need to remember the insights I've already had about teenaged boys. Your sons can probably attest to the fact that I am not the most patient man in the world, and when I find myself growing impatient, it is usually because I've forgotten something about teenaged boys that I already knew.

During the first semester of this school year I taught two classes, one of junior English and one of senior English. Long ago I learned that I cannot teach two classes and run a school, but that insight got lost in the need to cover a section of senior English. The senior English class was first period, and that gave me sometime before school to interact with the class on a more personal level than a teacher can do during the other periods in the day. Shortly after my December newsletter *On The Seasons Of Adolescence* hit the newsstands, one of the seniors commented, "Your newsletter this month was true. Sophomore year is really tough, and I was an idiot during it." At this there was general assent among the class that they had found sophomore year a rather trying experience, and another one of them commented, "I was such a punk during sophomore year."

I was overwhelmed by the fact that they had even read my newsletter, but more than that I was overwhelmed by a new realization of the very insight I had discussed in that letter. A few of the boys in that senior class had not had very good sophomore years, and I had carried into their senior year the impression that I had of them as sophomores. When I walked into the class on the first day, I looked around and thought to myself, "There are certainly a couple of punks in here. This could be a challenge." Of course, I discovered over the semester that the very boys that I thought were "punks" had turned into very fine young men and good students at that. They were an absolute delight to teach, and when I handed the class back to Mrs. Newcomb for the second semester, I was very sad to lose them. I know that teenaged boys mature tremendously between sophomore and senior year, but I had failed at first to give some of the young men in that class the benefit of my own insight. It is rather humbling to acknowledge that, try as I might and with twenty-five years of experience, I have not yet become the perfect school teacher.

Please don't get discouraged if you discover one day that you aren't the perfect parent. There are few, if any, perfect parents in the world just as there are very few perfect school teachers. Then again, there are very few perfect adolescents! Life has a way of reinforcing old insights and of teaching us to be patient with ourselves and with others. The theme of every retreat talk that I have ever given to students is that God doesn't look for results. God looks for effort. I don't think that God worries whether or not you are the perfect parent or I am the perfect school teacher. I do think, however, that He would be rather distressed with us if we stopped trying to be the perfect parent or the perfect school teacher. With our efforts, humble as they might be, and with His grace, things can't go too far wrong.

ON THE XAVERIAN PHILOSOPHY OF
EDUCATION AND BEGINNING WITH GOD

Creature of habit that I am, every year I begin my series of newsletters with a reflection on the Xaverian Brothers philosophy of education. As a religious community, we are 157 years old, and from 1839 until 1968 we were governed by two documents, our *Constitutions* and our *Manual of Customs and Advice.* Since most Brothers spent their lives in school, and since all Brothers were teaching only boys during those years, the documents reflect the Brothers' corporate wisdom on dealing with school boys. I'd like to share a few excerpts from these documents with you:

> The Brothers shall be neither too indulgent nor too severe with their pupils; they shall exercise over them a reasonable vigilance, at

the same time mild and paternal, but firm and active, without uneasiness or contention; they shall so exercise this vigilance that it may not be perceived by their pupils.

Let punishments, when they must be given to pupils, be moderate, just, reasonable and always proportionate to the fault. They must never be degrading or dishonoring. The Brothers shall take care never to lower the dignity of the man contained in the boy.

The Brothers shall not extract of their pupils too much perfection in their conduct in class but they shall avoid carefully any undue freedom and repress any disorder. They shall do their best to win the confidence and affection of their pupils, and with this objective view show interest in them, rejoicing or sympathizing with them like a good father in the midst of his family. They shall closely study the character of each pupil in order to guide him properly.

Endeavor to love those in your class who seem least lovable; try to moderate the natural affection you may feel for others.

Be just to all; let them have an equal share of your solicitude.

Speak to the pupils always respectfully, for they will respect you the more if you do so.

Unite the *suaviter in modo* with the *fortiter in re,* not permitting the least disorder; yet never

reprove or punish through caprice or fancy.
(Editor's note: For those whose Latin is rusty,
a very literal translation of *fortiter in re,
suaviter in modo* would be "The iron fist in
the velvet glove.")

Learn to make a distinction between those who
require an energetic remonstrance and those
who should be treated kindly and patiently.

I have always believed that teaching and parenting are two
sides of the same coin, and I'm sure that you recognize that
there is a great deal of parental wisdom contained in the Brothers' tradition. You may have one child who needs a great deal
of encouragement and a gentle approach to parenting while
you might have another child who tries you every step of the
way and who needs a rather tight leash. You make the distinction rather instinctively and know that you can't treat all of
your children exactly the same. Over the years I have been
impressed by how different two brothers can be, and I learned
long ago not to judge any young man by his brother. I remember one young man who walked into my classroom on the first
day and announced, "I'm Billy O'Rourke, and I'm nothing
like my brother. I'm a good kid." He wanted to make sure that
I didn't make the mistake of judging him by his brother who
was, indeed, a handful.

When I meet with new teachers after Mr. Sangalli has
hired them, I give them a little lesson on the Xaverian Brothers' approach to education. I tell them that we expect them
always to treat the boys respectfully even when the boys are
acting disrespectfully. In those situations they are always to
remember that they are the adults and that their students aren't
(at least not yet!). As young teachers, they need to use more of
the "iron fist" than the "velvet glove" until they have gained
good control of their classes. The tight leash can be loosened

when time and circumstances dictate. You probably used a much tighter leash with your first child as he or she went through adolescence than you have with your last child, You've learned a few tricks of the trade from your experience just as our young teachers will.

The last article in our *Manual of Customs and Advice* puts everything in its proper perspective, the perspective of eternity:

> Lastly, Brothers, bear in mind that your work in the classroom is God's and God's only. Man is but an instrument in His hands. Before class each day, pay a short visit to the Blessed Sacrament, acknowledge yourself to be but an instrument and remind the Lord that He can do good work with poor tools. Then depart for class fortified with His blessing. Do this, Brothers, and the work becomes God's. It will be yours in eternity.

That says it all, doesn't it? As parents and as teachers we are doing God's work. His help and guidance are readily available to us. All we have to do is ask. You have probably discovered by now that prayer is a necessity for the parents of a teenager. I can assure you that it's a necessity for a school president. As we begin this new school year, let's pray for one another and for all the young men who will be educated at St. X this year. The school year, then, will become God's, and if He is present, all will be well.

ON PHYSICAL AND EMOTIONAL MATURITY

When Danny walked into my classroom at the beginning of his freshman year, he stood 6' 4" and had a beard that was heavier than that of most of the men on the faculty. I thought that perhaps a senior had misread his schedule, but since I had never seen Danny about the school, I concluded that he had to be a freshman, a very large freshman, but nevertheless a freshman. Despite his size, he was very much a fourteen year old with the spontaneity and enthusiasm which make freshmen such a delight to teach. The drinking age in those days was eighteen, and I'm sure that Danny could have been served in any bar without any question, but in my classroom he was about as typical a freshman as you can get. During his sophomore year he asked to see me, and I was quite surprised to find him rather upset. He was always very even-tempered. It seems he had asked to be moved up in Spanish for his sophomore year, and now he found himself over his head. His mother suggested that he come to see me because I would know that he was a hard worker and not just slacking off.

"You know I work hard, Brother, and I'm really trying," he said, "but I just can't do it." With that his eyes welled with tears, and I was struck very forcefully by the fact that I was looking at a man and talking to a boy. As Shakespeare pointed out in much of his work, appearance and reality are frequently not the same thing.

What's the point? You have probably discovered by now that adolescent males mature physically much more quickly than they mature emotionally and psychologically. Your son may look like a man, but he will remind you very frequently that he hasn't quite caught up with his body. The "not a boy but not yet a man" syndrome is part and parcel of adolescence with a male. You might consider it the "ugly duckling" stage. When it ends, you have a man both in body and in spirit, but the process can be rather confusing for parents.

It is this body/spirit tension which gets teenaged males into the most trouble. People who deal with adolescent males, their teachers and their parents, can at times assume that they are as mature as they look. When teachers and parents make that assumption, the young men then find very creative ways to disabuse us of that false impression. You, for example, might think your son is certainly old enough and mature enough to remain at home unchaperoned while you take a trip. I would be the first to admit that there are some teenagers who are mature enough to handle that responsibility, but, if I were a parent, I wouldn't press my luck. I've known too many parents who have returned from a romantic weekend to find their house in a shambles and the local police pounding on the door. That's just one example, but I'm sure you can think of many more. Or perhaps you'd rather not think of any! There's very little that you and I can do at this stage in a young man's life. He simply has to grow through it until his mind catches up with his body. Actually, you can pray. What you can't control, you had best put in God's hands.

On those days when the man standing in front of you acts like a boy, don't get discouraged. It's that difficult in-between stage, and it will pass. Just remember that your son needs a great deal of support during this time. He's as confused by this tension between his body and his mind as you are. In time his mind will catch up with his body, and he'll be a man physically and psychologically. I'll bet you can't wait for that day!

ON YOUR SON AND SEX

I need to warn you that I'm going to be a bit more blunt than I normally am in my letters to you. I'm afraid that the topic of the adolescent and sex does not lend itself to subtlety, but there are some things regarding this topic that I need to say and that you need to hear.

When I began my teaching career in 1971, I was assigned to teach two periods of junior religion in a course entitled "Love, Sex and Marriage." I had entered religious life six days after my eighteenth birthday, and my experience with regard to the topic of this religion course was absolutely nonexistent, but in those long ago days we were still living under the illusion that the Brothers should be teaching the religion courses in school even if the Brothers were not terribly conversant with the subject matter. On the day I decided to tackle the chapter in their textbook on sexual intercourse, I did a particularly atrocious job of teaching the material. Embarrassed and unsure of myself, I made no sense, and the class clown decided to point that out. In a moment of extreme frustration I said, "Well, when the time comes, you'll figure it out." Definitely the wrong thing to say! That became the watchword for the rest of the school year. Whenever I would get confused, they would clamor in unison, "Don't worry, Brother, when the time comes, we'll figure it out." When we got to the chapter on why they should abstain from premarital sex, the same class clown commented, "Will somebody tell the poor man that it's too late."

I've learned a lot since then about adolescent bragging rights and sex, and I suspect that then there were far more boys in the class who would like their classmates to believe that they were sexually active than there actually were. On the other hand, there probably were a good number of boys in the class who were indeed already sexually active.

Every Catholic high school that I've been associated with teaches Christian sexual morality quite clearly and quite emphatically: Abstinence until marriage. Everything else, however, that the young men encounter in their life and in society stands in opposition to what they've been taught at home and in school. All too frequently parents avoid talking to their sons about sex because it's a difficult topic to approach under the best of circumstances, and frequently parents are finally driven to talk about it in less than ideal circumstances when something has gone drastically wrong. I'd like to suggest that you tackle the topic with your son before the proverbial horse is out of the barn. Perhaps he'll listen to you, and you'll save yourself and him a lot of heartache. Perhaps he won't. Nothing ventured, nothing gained. I might add here that if you do talk to your son about sex, you need to be incredibly explicit. The "birds and the bees" doesn't hack it anymore. Teenaged males don't understand subtlety, and if you have any hope of getting through to your son, you can't be subtle.

The sexual scene with adolescents has changed dramatically in the past twenty years. When I was a boy, the worst thing that could happen was that your girlfriend got pregnant. In these days of AIDS, death is the worst thing that can happen. Adolescents with AIDS are an increasing phenomenon, and since adolescent sex is not usually planned because adolescents don't plan anything, they tend not to take precautions, increasing their risks in a number of areas.

Up until this year, in Kentucky as in many other states, we couldn't give your son an aspirin at school without your permission, but he could accompany his girlfriend to an abortion clinic and, without any parental consent, end a pregnancy. You need to pray daily that if your son ever finds himself in a difficult position, he will come to you first before he tries to do anything about it. I can't tell you how many times I've spoken to students whose girlfriends are pregnant and told them that their parents will understand if only they trust them enough to tell them. I can say quite honestly that I've never had a parent let me down in that regard. If I can get the boy to talk with them, they do their best to understand.

A few years ago I had a young man in class who went through a total change of personality within a week. Being the dutiful school teacher, I called him into my office and asked him what the problem was. He claimed that there was nothing wrong. Fortunately the Holy Spirit was with me, and I asked if his girlfriend were pregnant. He replied most emphatically that she wasn't. I would have stopped there, but again the Holy Spirit prompted me to ask, "Was she?" The floodgates fell, and the boy began to cry uncontrollably, "I didn't know what else to do. We're too young to be parents." I knew the boy's parents very well, and I knew that if he had only told them, they would have understood and would have helped him. Unfortunately he tried to tackle the problem on his own. It wasn't that he didn't know that what he did was seriously sinful. He knew quite clearly that it was. Adolescent that he was, he felt trapped, and he acted very much against his conscience. When

I suggested to him that he needed to see Father Dennis, the school chaplain, he looked at me somewhat quizzically and said, "It couldn't be that simple. It couldn't be that simple for God to forgive me." I assured him that God's forgiveness was absolutely no problem. Forgiving himself was going to be the tough part.

What's the moral of all this? St. Xavier High School can teach your son all of the Christian moral principles that he needs to know, but those principles are not going to become part of his life unless they are reinforced at home. A teenaged boy is at the height of his sexual drive. His hormones do things to him that he doesn't really understand, and he needs you, his parents, to help him understand. I remember a father who once came to ask if I would talk to his son about sex. He was convinced that his son was sexually active, and he was sure that his son was not taking any precautions. He said, "I'm his father. He won't listen to me, but he likes you. He'll listen to you." I replied, "I like your son very much too, and I'd be proud to be his father, but I'm not. You are. I'm afraid this is your job, not mine."

Do you get my drift? As you talk with your son about sex, you'll be embarrassed, and he'll be embarrassed. Then again, you might just keep him alive and out of trouble. We at St. X will do whatever we can to help you in dealing with your son with this difficult topic. Our guidance counselors are more than ready to assist you in any way that they can. Your son's health and well-being are very important to us. Just like you, we want to keep him alive and out of trouble.

ON TRUSTING THAT GOD WILL DO HIS BEST

Twenty-five years ago I began my teaching career at St. John's High School, and during each of the three years I taught at St. John's, I had Jimmy Coggins as a student in either Latin or religion. Jimmy was an incredibly quiet boy, the oldest child in a family of seven children. I came to know his family rather well in those years. Jim, the father, was about as devout a Catholic as there has ever been but in a remarkably unpretentious way. The administrator of a large Catholic hospital, he attended Mass every day of his life.

I remember Jimmy taking me on one day after religion class. He just wasn't buying my attempts at making religion "relevant." "Now my dad is a real Catholic," he said. "They don't make them like him anymore. Mass every day. The rosary. He's just a really good man. None of this stuff you're teaching us." I knew the father so I had no defense against the son. Jimmy was right on the mark, and I was batting out fungos.

Religious that I was, I felt lukewarm and convictionless next to Jim Coggins.

I kept in touch with Jimmy and the Coggins family after I left St. John's. Jimmy attended my final vow ceremony, and I was at his wedding. By sheer coincidence, I was in Worcester the day that Jimmy Coggins died. He was only twenty-seven years old, and his death was sudden. He left behind a pregnant wife and a son. As soon as I heard of his death, I went to see his parents. I have had far too much experience with parents grieving for a son, but in this instance, I didn't have my role as principal and religious to support me. Jim Coggins was old enough to be my father, and, in many ways, he had treated me as if I were a son. As for faith, mine was only a very pale shadow next to his. On that very sad morning, Jim was the consoler. His consolation was his faith, a faith that he had passed on to his son. It seems that about a month before he died, Jimmy had begun to attend the early morning Mass at Holy Rosary Church. He brought his own infant son with him and quietly joined his father in this very important part of Jim's daily routine. Knowing Jim and Jimmy, I can picture the father, the son and the grandson at morning Mass. I'm sure that there weren't many words apart from whatever sounds Jimmy's son chose to make. Jim and Jimmy were men of few words.

As I reflect on these two men, I am reminded of how many times I have heard parents tell me, "We sent our children to Catholic schools. We tried to bring them up in the faith, and now they never go to Mass." I'm reminded of how many times as a religion teacher I have become discouraged by the number of my former students who seem to have fallen away from their faith. At those times, I try to tell the parents and myself what I have come to believe is true. Our job is to plant the seed of faith and to water that seed as best we can. At times we may do a rotten job of it, but then we have to remember that God looks at intentions and not at results. Our job is to plant the seed. God's job is to bring the seed to fruition. Fortunately He has more patience than we do, and He sees more clearly into the heart than ever we could. It would be nice to see the seed flower as Jim Coggins did in the last month of his son's life, but even if we aren't granted that privilege, we have to believe that God, in His own good time, will see that His job is done.

Jim Coggins died less than a year after his son. At the funeral his second son, Jack, spoke eloquently about what it was like for his brothers and sister to grow up "in my father's house." After a moving tribute to this man of tremendous faith, Jack concluded his eulogy, "And now my father is with my brother in his Father's house where he always longed to be."

You and I may not have the faith of Jim Coggins. We may not even come close. When it comes to passing on our faith to our sons and our students, we can only do our best knowing that God will do His. And if God is doing His best, we don't have to worry.

ON HEARING WHAT YOUR SON IS NOT SAYING

If your son talks with you frequently sharing the ups and downs of his day and his life, you should be on your knees nightly thanking God for a truly miraculous blessing. Most teenaged boys are not good communicators. It isn't that they don't feel deeply. They do, but rarely can they find the words to express what is going on inside them. The good parent and the good school teacher have to become somewhat intuitive when trying to communicate with a teenaged boy. You have to listen carefully to the silence and intuit the meaning. This is no easy task, and I can tell you that after twenty-five years of dealing with teenaged boys, it's an art that I have not completely mastered. Some days I can be right on the money, interpreting beautifully what is going on inside one of my students, and on other days I can miss completely the unspoken message. I'm sure that you've had the same experience.

Adolescence is an incredibly confusing time, and

most teenaged boys can't make any sense of all that is going on inside of them. The more deeply they feel about anything, the more difficulty they have articulating it. They sense things going on inside of them, but they can't name these feelings. Their frustration at not being able to articulate or to name all that they feel can lead them to give their parents and their teachers very contradictory signals.

If you haven't learned it yet, you need to learn Kelly's rule for interpreting what teenaged boys are saying. The rule is never take what they say or do at face value. When you've caught your son doing something he shouldn't and he tells you that he hates you or that he's sick of your interfering in his life, what he probably means is "Thank God you finally figured it all out and stopped me. I was getting in over my head, and I was scared to death, and I didn't know what to do." When a senior who has had a very positive experience at St. X says in March of his senior year that he's tired of St. X and all its rules and that he can't wait to leave, he is probably saying, "This has been such a safe and secure place for me. What am I ever going to do when I have to leave here?" A teenaged boy who tells you, "Get off my case" could well be saying, "Please stay on my case because if you do that, I know that you love me." It's all very confusing!

I couldn't possibly discuss adolescent communication with you without touching upon the two D's: Death and Divorce. If a teenaged boy tells you when he has experienced either of these realities that he is just fine, he's not telling you the truth. He's not lying because he thinks that he is fine. Believe me, he isn't. You need to find opportunities for him to deal with his feelings in a safe environment. He may not take the opportunity, but he has to know that it's there. Whether you offer him professional counseling or a shoulder to cry on, he needs to know that he has the option.

There are times when teenagers take absolute delight in confusing adults and in giving them mixed signals. Let me give you a brief example from my own experience. I'm a very passionate teacher, and I have the good fortune of loving what I teach. I am particularly fond of the Romantic Poets in English Literature, and every year I get overly enthusiastic when we come to the Romantic Poets and to my favorite of the Romantics, John Keats. Last year as I was waxing eloquently, my class seemed to be in complete torpor. At one point I could repress my frustration no longer, and I exclaimed, "Do you think that you guys could give me a break here? I love this stuff, and you're giving me no reaction. You sit there with these bored looks on your face almost defying me to teach you." Well, they didn't want to tick me off because that would cause them more grief than they were prepared to endure, so they roused themselves slightly from their torpor and began to answer my questions. I gave a great school teacherly sigh and went on with the lesson. At the end of the year the English Department decided to adopt a new text in English literature, and Ms. Reisert, Chair of the English Department, asked each teacher to provide three boys with different learning styles to evaluate the new text. After the textbook choice had been made, I asked one of the students in my class who was on the committee why he had rejected a particular text. He answered immediately, "It didn't have nearly enough selection by the Romantic Poets, and certainly it didn't have enough of Keats." Dumbfounded, I asked him if he enjoyed the Romantic Poets. Realizing that I had caught him, he gave me that enigmatic teenage smile and said, "Yea, I do." When I asked why he hadn't made that obvious to me when I was teaching the Romantics, he smiled again and shrugged as if to suggest that it was good for my humility if he and his classmates didn't give me too much encouragement.

Don't get discouraged if you get no response when you try to communicate with your son. Don't get discouraged but don't stop trying. Listen carefully to the silence and learn, as best you can, to intuit the meaning. When you do intuit

137

correctly, let him know that you have figured out what he isn't saying. It's good for his humility, and, while he'll never admit it, it lets him know that he doesn't have the upper hand completely. And you thought your own adolescence was confusing!

ON THE GILBERTS AND TAKING TIME

George and Joan Gilbert had eleven children, ten boys and one girl, that included three sets of twins. They put all ten of their boys through Xavier High School in Connecticut, and it was my privilege, when the last one graduated, to bestow an honorary diploma on George and Joan. To my knowledge, Joan is the only woman to hold a Xavier High School diploma. I wanted to honor them at graduation not simply because they had managed the incredible feat of almost twenty years of tuition but because they were, for me and for many, a model of good parenting. I often thought that if Joan and George could bottle their parenting recipe, they could make a fortune.

I taught four of the Gilberts, and I was the principal of the school when the last two graduated. There wasn't a bad kid in the lot of them, and I was frequently assured by the members of the faculty that the first four whom I missed were as nice as their brothers. Imagine ten brothers and not a bad one in the lot! I don't think that this happened by accident, and I often wondered what it was that George and Joan had done to mold such fine sons. I think that I got a hint of their secret when the last boy was a freshman.

George and Joan came to everything. They made every P.T.A., and they were at any school event in which one of their sons was involved and at many school events when none of their sons were involved. When their last son was a freshman, I was watching a cross country meet in which Mark was running. Of course, there was George. Joan, if I recall correctly, was at Mercy High School at some event at which their only daughter was involved. I asked George how many cross country meets, swim meets and school plays he had seen in his career. He laughed and then gave me a bit of insight into his skills as a parent. He said, "When Joan and I decided that we were going to have a big family, we promised ourselves that we would give the last one the same time and attention that we had given the first one." Time and attention! George and Joan Gilbert had given all of their children time and attention, and it showed. The Gilbert boys were all very different, even the twins. They all, however, had a good sense of themselves and a sense of security which, in my humble opinion, came from the time and the attention which their parents had given them.

I don't think that it's possible for you as parents to give your children too much of your time and your attention if you do it in a way that is not overprotective. Your son, being a typical teenager, will lead you to believe that he doesn't want your time and attention, and he may even growl at you when you try to give it to him. I can assure you, however, that he wants it and he needs it despite what he says. I would remind you again of one of Kelly's primary rules of dealing with teenaged boys: Never take what they say at face value. They usually don't mean it. In fact, they usually don't know what they mean.

You need to make time in your life for whatever is going on in your son's life. You may not be able to attend every activity in which he's involved, but you should make your presence at these events a regular occurrence. You need to spend time with him just talking which is a formidable task since teenaged boys tend not to be very communicative. However you accomplish it, your son needs to know how very important he is to you. If he knows that and if he knows that you'll love him even when he's not being very lovable, he has a far better chance of growing into a mature man than he would without those reassurances.

I remember one retreat closing when a young man felt obliged to explain to the crowd why his mother wasn't there. She had a good reason, but as he looked out at all of the other retreatants' mothers, he felt the need to explain. I recall one young man who said to me quite matter-of-factly, "My father is always around to share in the glory when I do well in sports, but he's never there when I really need him." The mother probably didn't realize how very important it was to her son that she be present at his retreat closing, and the father probably didn't know how his son perceived their relationship. I think the Gilberts would have known those things simply because of the amount of time and attention they gave to their children.

Hopefully, I have communicated to you frequently enough my firm conviction that God does not expect you to be perfect parents or me to be the perfect school president. He does expect us to try to be those things. Nonetheless, we have to take our lessons from those who can teach with experience. Since I'm supposed to be the spiritual father of this little corner of God's kingdom, I try to attend as many extracurricular events at St. X as I can. It's a lesson I learned from George Gilbert. I hope it helps you.

ON VIGILANCE

The Brother must be ever alert to any danger to the spiritual as well as the physical welfare of his charges. He is a visible Guardian Angel in his watchfulness over them. Prudently aware of their friendships, their conversations and their tendencies in reading and recreation, he can enjoy by his unceasing solicitude the consolation of preserving the innocence of their lives.
—From the Manual of Customs and
Advice of the Xaverian Brothers

Four years ago the Louisville Police told us that drugs were going to become rampant very shortly within the Louisville high school scene. Their prediction, unfortunately, proved true. Now they tell us that within four years we will see a serious increase in gang activity. While I hope that their prediction will not come true, it probably will. Adolescents today are confronted with far more temptations than were their parents and even their older brothers and sisters. It's a sad fact of life, but it is a fact of life of which you as parents and we as educators have to be actively aware.

Not long ago we had some serious incidents with drugs, and in the middle of Mr. Sangalli's dealing with these problems, a young man was sent to the office for talking back to a teacher. As I watched the scene develop, I was painfully aware of how things had changed. The boy who had spoken back to the teacher was "small potatoes" in the ebb and flow of school discipline on that day. I remember when he would have headed the list. Obviously things have not changed for the better.

Please pardon me if what follows is repetitious. Those of you who have had sons in school for four years have heard all of this before, but it bears repeating. Given the temptations which adolescents face today, you as parents need to be incredibly vigilant, perhaps far more vigilant than your own parents were with you. The trouble that you and I could get into when we were teenagers is unfortunately "small potatoes" compared to the trouble which teenagers can get into today.

WHERE? WHY? WHEN? HOW LONG? WITH WHOM? These are all questions that you need answered whenever your son leaves the house. You need to know where he is going and with whom he's going. Make sure that you get to know your son's friends, and if possible, get to know the parents of his friends. As his parents who are providing him with his education and paying his bills, you have a right to know what he's up to. If your son is a typical teenaged boy, he will be quite reticent in sharing this information, but you are perfectly within your rights to expect him to let you know where he's going and what he's doing. There is an incredible parental balancing act here. If you are too strict, you could drive him into open rebellion, and if you are too loose, you risk his falling in with the wrong crowd in the wrong place at the wrong time. Do your best to keep the lines of communication open but also realize that, as his parents, you need to draw the line at times to protect him from himself.

I wish that I could guarantee you that during his four years at St. X, your son will never run into another boy who is a bad influence on him, but I can't guarantee that. Every day fourteen hundred young men come to the St. X campus, and they bring with them all the influences of the world in which they live. We do our best daily to dam the flood of the human potential and to keep your sons on the straight and narrow. I think we do as fine a job at that as a school can. We are very clear with your sons about what we will tolerate and what we won't, and we are very clear on the consequences of doing what we won't tolerate. I hope that we never act without compassion, but we have to be vigilant for the entire student body. If at times we take a hard line, we do so to protect and to teach the student body as a whole. This has been part of the Xaverian Brothers' philosophy of education since the beginning, and in our old rule there was actually an article on the dismissal of boys from school. The rule recognized that some boys could be bad influences on other boys and that the Brothers' first obligation was to protect the majority. Every time Mr. Sangalli has to dismiss a student, my heart goes out both to Mr. Sangalli and to the boy because I know that it is a painful experience for both of them. I was a principal for nine years, and the dismissal of students was one aspect of the job that I very much disliked.

Those of you who grew up in the pre-Vatican II Church perhaps remember St. Dominic Savio, the teenage saint. Saint Dominic lived from 1842-1857. He was apparently an incredibly virtuous young man and a wonderful role model for his friends. In my twenty-five years in school, I have met countless wonderful young men, but I've never met Saint Dominic Savio because I've never met a teenager, even the best of them, who did not have the ability to make serious mistakes. Adolescent boys are great experimenters. Unfortunately at times they can experiment in ways that are wholly unacceptable and very dangerous. Because they haven't lived as long as we have, they don't see the consequences looming, and they don't think before they act. Since they tend not to be vigilant themselves, you and I need to be vigilant for them. We need to do what we can as parents and school teachers to foresee the problems that might be on the horizon and to do whatever we can to alert our sons and our students to the real dangers which confront them. Perhaps they'll listen, and we'll save them and ourselves a great deal of heartache. Perhaps they won't, but the possible consequences of not trying to alert them are rather frightening.

I realize that this letter is far more somber than my usual monthly reflections to you. I worry a lot more about the boys at St. X than I used to worry about any of my students. There are far too many temptations out there, and they're young and inexperienced. Be as vigilant as you can for your son's well-being and pray for him with all your heart everyday. I have to admit that I pray a lot more than I used to. My prayer is always very simple: Dear God, keep them safe and out of harm's way. I like to remind God that, once I've done all I can, it's His job to do what I can't.

Pray for spring.

ON TACT AND THE ANTITHETICAL
NATURE OF THE ADOLESCENT MALE

Once long ago, I tactlessly asked a woman if she were her
son's grandmother. She took it rather well I thought. At least
she didn't hit me. Now, even if a woman appears to be 102, I
ask if she's the boy's mother. I've made a lot of grandmothers
happy in recent years. Those who know me best will tell you
right readily that tact has never been my strongest suit. When
pressed, I am as apt to tell parents that their son is a spoiled
brat as I am to suggest more tactfully that just maybe, perhaps their son has gotten a bit too used to having his own
way. Quite frankly I prefer the former, but some parents
don't appreciate such a forthright assessment from the head
of their son's school. The comments which appear next to
your son's grades on his report card are rather matter-of-
factly tactful. His grade is poor because his homework isn't
done, or his grade is excellent because he is a hard-work-

ing young man. Since we try to be tactful, report card comments can't really cut to the heart of the matter. Here are a few comments which you will never see on your son's report card but which might more accurately assess a boy in the process of becoming a man.

"Kissed the blarney stone. Thinks his charm will get him through life."
"Less whining. More work."
"Hormones out of control. Put him on a tight leash."
"Social butterfly. Needs wings clipped."
"Much too shy. Needs girlfriend. Give him the car keys and send him to one of the girls' schools for a visit."
"Thinks life is going to provide him with a free lunch."
"Nice boy, but lazy as sin."
"Too responsible. Needs to be a kid."
"Has all the answers. Unfortunately none of them are to the questions his teachers are asking."
"Has more excuses than Carter has Little Liver Pills."
"Looking a bit seedy lately. Substance abuse could be looming on the horizon."
"Passes by classroom at 3 p.m., waves at the teacher and then claims that he's gone for extra help."
"Needs a bit more freedom."
"Needs some clearer boundaries. Send him to his room until he's 30!"

The challenge of working with teenaged boys is that they never change and they always change. One minute I can be railing at a boy for his laziness and irresponsibility, and fifteen minutes later I can be encouraging another boy to lighten up and to be less serious about life and his school work. One day I may tell a given set of parents that their son is out of control, and the next day tell another set of parents that their son is under far too much pressure and needs some space. The common denominator in all of these instances is adolescence.

Your son's adolescence is a difficult time for him and a trying time for you. No boy or parent gets through it without bumps and bruises. At times he will dislike you intensely, and you won't much like him. At those times it is important to remember that "liking" has nothing to do with love. It's also important to remember that adolescence is just a (relatively) brief sojourn on the road to manhood. Your son will survive his adolescence, and with a great deal of prayer and patience, so will you.

The grass, of course, is always greener in the other parent's yard. You'd probably love to see "too responsible" as a comment on your son's report card. Dream on! Living with a male adolescent is God's way of keeping you on your toes. If your son has anything to say about it, your life won't be dull.

Is it spring yet?

ON KNOWING WHEN TO APOLOGIZE

Recently I received a call from a young man who graduated from Xavier High School in Connecticut in 1988 inviting me to his wedding. A school teacher always loves to be remembered by former students, and I was touched at the invitation. I remembered him well because during his senior year he had, on one sad day, received the brunt of one of my greatest overreactions to a teenager in my career as a school administrator. I was passing a classroom at the very moment that he was being incredibly rude to the revered Mrs. Hancock. It would be like a St. X senior being rude to Mrs. Newcomb or Ms. Rapier. I went ballistic, hauled him out of the classroom and chased him out of the school (literally!) hollering all the while that he would never graduate from Xavier High School. About two hours after this scene which was heard by the entire senior hallway, an assistant principal came into my office and told me that Chuck was sitting on the front steps of the school. I

149

went out, and Chuck began our very brief conversation:

"I'm sorry. I was really stupid."
"I'm sorry, too. I overreacted."
"Can I come back now?"
"If you apologize to Mrs. Hancock and spend at least a week in jug."
"Deal!"

Both Chuck and I learned a lesson, and since I was delighted to be invited to his wedding, I guess neither of us has held a grudge.

You have probably discovered that you deal with adolescence best if you have vast reservoirs of patience. Unfortunately, for most parents and for most school teachers, the reservoir occasionally runs dry, and when that happens, the adolescent can find himself on the losing end of a burst of temper. Now that's not necessarily a bad position for an adolescent to be in. I've always felt that a very clear shot across the bow can be a rather sobering moment for a teenaged boy, and in my career I've fired off more of these shots across the bow than I could possibly ever remember. There are, however, those times when the shot across the bow is really undeserved or a little stronger than it needs to be. Yes, it's sad to say, but we adults at times can overreact to teenagers. As his mother or his father or the head of his high school, you and I probably love him dearly, but there will be those days when adolescent exuberance or adolescent insensitivity or adolescent failure to think of the consequences will push us over the edge into overreaction. Think of this momentary loss of patience as a wonderful chance to practice humility.

I don't know if it's something I learned from my parents or if it's just a natural outgrowth of my at times irascible Irish disposition, but I've never had any trouble apologizing for my mistakes. I've apologized at times to kids, to classes, to the faculty and on a couple of occasions to the entire school. To admit one's mistakes and to make amends where possible is just about the best lesson we adults can teach kids. Of course, we can only teach this very important lesson by example. When you or I overreact with our sons or students, we need to recognize that fact by apologizing sincerely and by making whatever amends are necessary. That doesn't mean that we overlook the offense that pushed us over the edge, nor does it mean that we can't assign a punishment commensurate with the offense. It simply means that we have to say that we're sorry and to acknowledge that the offense did not deserve the reaction.

Recently, I took one of our freshmen on for a fare-thee-well, and after I had sent him on his way, I felt that I had probably overreacted. It wouldn't have been an overreaction for an upperclassman, but freshmen are still learning the St. X ropes. I called the boy to tell him that I was sorry that I had overreacted, but he wasn't home so I left a message on his family's answering machine. I received a call back from his father who told me that I shouldn't be apologizing to his son and that his son had probably done whatever it was I thought he did. Now, that's my kind of parent! I did, however, still meet with the boy the following Monday so that he could understand why I was angry with him. The beautiful thing about teenaged boys is that they are very quick to forgive and forget. Holding grudges is not a "boy thing." One Friday when the Board of Directors was in school, I snapped at my class because they did not have their homework done as well as I would have liked. Again, Irish guilt overtook me, and on Monday I apologized for my overreaction. One lad immediately said, "That's O.K., Brother. We know that you're always a little tense when the Board is in the building." They had figured me out before I had figured myself out, and they were quite willing to forgive me for my overreaction.

Don't become impatient with yourself when you become impatient with your son. Such impatience is an unavoidable aspect of parenting. Do have the humility to apologize when you are wrong. Your son may or may not receive the apology graciously, but he will learn a very positive lesson for that (hopefully) far off day when he has lost patience with his own son. Of course, at that point you will be far too busy spoiling your grandson to worry about your son's reactions to anything!

ON COMPLETING THE TASK

On August 30, 1993, three hundred and fifty insecure four-teen-year-old boys entered St. Xavier as the Class of 1997. With quiet determination the faculty set about their task of molding this rather diverse group of boys into a class of confident and capable men. Of course, the faculty wasn't alone in their task. They had the cooperation of the parents of these boys, and since the faculty are all Catholic educators, they knew that God would be present in the process with the grace of His Holy Spirit. Nonetheless, it was a formidable task. Three and a half years later during the spring semester as the Class of 1997 prepared to graduate, we had some very clear signs that the faculty had not labored in vain. Let me share with you a few of those signs that the Class of 1997 had learned what St. X had to teach.

The Ascension Thursday Mass became an incredible

moment of grace for the St. X community. Senior David Wills had been asked to give a reflection at the Mass, and he chose the Gospel of the Prodigal Son. David was well prepared, and his reflection was magnificent. He was talking to an audience that was 99% male, all of whom had some experience of the trickiness of the father-son relationship. As David spoke, you could see the prodigal son come alive in the eyes of the student body, and you could see recognition in those eyes, recognition that at times each one of us has been the prodigal son. From my unique perspective sitting on the altar, I watched the reaction of the student body to one of their peers. I don't think any adult on that day could have moved them more deeply than David did. Even more beautiful to behold was Miss Keene sitting in the last row bursting with pride as she watched one of her former EXCEL boys, now a confident young man, hold the rapt attention of the school. The music at the Mass was as fine as David's talk. Mr. Knoop had the Tiger Chorus perfectly prepared for the liturgy, and they sang beautifully. As a Communion reflection, the chorus sang *Wade in the Water,* an upbeat spiritual, and seniors Danny Shoemaker and Sean Fore took solo parts. Danny and Sean, confident in their talent, sang with a depth of feeling which moved the entire school. For the rest of the day, I heard boys humming that song in the hallways as they changed classes.

In the last weeks of school, Nick Rainey set about collecting money from all of the students in Mrs. Newcomb's classes so that all of her students might give her a very special gift as she retires after twenty-six years as a teacher at St. X. Nick bought a beautiful *Complete Works of William Shakespeare* which he had all of her students sign, a thoughtful tribute on the part of thoughtful students for a revered teacher.

It is the custom at St. X that the student speaker at graduation be chosen by a committee of seniors and teachers. Any student can prepare a graduation address to be delivered to this committee which makes the choice of a speaker. This year we had sixteen seniors prepare graduation addresses, and Brother George, the Chairman of the committee, told me that all sixteen of the speeches were excellent and worthy of graduation. "There wasn't one of them," he said, "which would not make us proud if it were delivered at graduation." The committee chose Brian Derhake to give the graduation address, and as Brother George had predicted, Brian certainly made us proud. I would like to share with you a few of his remarks.

> At St. X, academic and extracurricular excellence has been stressed, but we soon found that there is a much deeper side to life. Through our retreat program, we were united as a class, forgetting our differences and becoming united. Many of us "fell in love with the service of God," leading us to the formation of the Ryken Service Club which is named after Theodore Ryken the founder of the Xaverian Brothers and which provided more hours of community service in the first semester of this year than any previous class has provided in an entire year.... Throughout our four years, we have received countless awards, measuring our excellence for all to see. Our mark was made when we found out our class contained nineteen National Merit Semi-Finalists. Our mark was made when several athletes received the "All American" status. Our mark was made in our excellent drama performances and our band and choir concerts. As we leave St. X, we will remember some of these extraordinary awards, but more

than likely, the vast majority of our memories will be of the people whom we have
come to know and the experiences we have
shared.

Brian's graduation address indicated that he has come
to understand quite clearly the values which St. X has held
dear for the past 133 years. The school has always encouraged
excellence but not in a vacuum. The values of our faith, the
values of the Gospel require service. The Class of 1997 seems
to have learned that lesson and, hopefully, will continue to
use the many talents God has given them for the benefit of
their fellow human beings. I like to think that on graduation day, Brother Paul, the founder of St. X, was smiling
down from heaven at the graduating class, thinking to himself, "Now these young men are just what I had in mind
133 years ago when I founded St. X. They are Christian
gentlemen who are going to make a difference in the world."

St. X has completed its task with the Class of 1997,
and we send them forth, proud of all that they have accomplished and confident that they will, indeed, make a difference
in the world.

ON EXPECTING THE BEST AND
MEANING WHAT YOU SAY
WHEN YOU EXPECT THE BEST

I was taught in high school by the Sisters of Saint Joseph of Boston, a formidable group of women. My good friend, Brother Raymond, is also a product of "Josie" education, and when we were stationed together in Connecticut, we had a theoretical question we would ask each other on those occasions when the boys were being particularly antsy, like the last day before Christmas vacation when the sky was threatening snow. The question was "How many Sisters of St. Joseph of Boston would it take to keep these kids in line?" The answer was always one, and she'd do it by raising her eyebrows. In the days when all you could see of a nun was her face, a Sister of Saint Joseph could quell a riot with a frown. The nuns who taught me acted as if they were born to rule, and rule they did. Their classroom was their kingdom, and within the walls of their classroom their authority was absolute. These women set high standards and expected their students to meet them. Settling for second best was never an option.

When I think about the Sisters who taught me in high school, I remember them with profound gratitude. They saw potential in an incredibly lazy fourteen-year-old boy, and they wouldn't leave me alone until I began to live up to that potential. They did the same for all of my classmates. Without our being aware of it, we began to see ourselves and our potentials through the nuns' eyes, and we began to realize those potentials. In a very real sense they made us believe in ourselves. But they didn't do it gently!

When I entered the Brothers, I saw in the Xaverians the same incredible dedication to their students that I experienced in the Sisters of Saint Joseph of Boston. As a young Brother in the classroom, I learned early that my job was to expect nothing but the best from my students, and if I expected nothing but the best, they'd produce it. I recall one evening sitting in the common room at St. John's High School correcting papers when the Superior, Brother Ivan, noticed that one boy had turned in an incredibly sloppy piece of work to me. Brother Ivan seized the teachable moment and said, "Never accept work like that from a boy. You hand that back to him tomorrow and tell him that it's an insult to his intelligence and to you as his teacher." I was rather astounded when the boy handed me a very fine piece of work two days later. Brother Ivan wanted me to know that if I expected nothing but the best, my students would generally produce it. There is a great deal of truth in Brother Ivan's attitude. If you set high standards with teenaged boys, they usually rise to the occasion.

Unfortunately, boys will only rise to the high standards if they are absolutely sure that the person setting the standards has no intention of backing off from them. Boys always look for the loopholes, and if, when setting standards for them, you don't really mean what you say, they will intuit that immediately and respond appropriately. I've learned over the years that if you are going to deal with teenaged boys effectively, you need always to mean what you say and to hold your ground once you've said it. If "I'm grounding you for two weeks" really means "I'm grounding you until you drive me so crazy with your whining that I give in," your son will make sure that the two weeks becomes two days or even less An adult dealing with a male adolescent has to keep his or her eye on the long-term goals. Enduring the torture which comes from living with an adolescent who has been grounded for two weeks is a small price to pay to establish in that adolescent's mind that you mean what you say. Nothing undermines an adult's authority with an adolescent more quickly than idle threats which the adult doesn't mean and can't or won't enforce. Set your expectations for your son high, but be sure they are sufficiently reasonable so that he can actually meet them. Once you've set high and reasonable expectations, don't back off!

As we begin this school year, I think that we, parents and teachers, need to set the standards high for the 1,400 young men who will be educated at St. X this year. They will whine and complain as teenaged boys do whenever they are presented with something difficult to do, but most of them will rise to the occasion. St. X is the wonderful institution it is today because for 133 years the Xaverian Brothers and our lay colleagues have been expecting nothing but the best from St. X students. They haven't disappointed us. Perhaps some incredibly lazy fourteen-year-old boy in the Class of 2001 may become a school president one day. Stranger things have happened!

ON FIGHTS AND THE COMPETITIVE NATURE
OF THE ADOLESCENT MALE

Once upon a time, in a Xaverian school far away, a fight broke out in the cafeteria between one of the school bullies and a boy of no particular pugilistic ability. The Brother prefecting the cafeteria observed from a distance that the bully was getting the stuffing beaten out of him. Responding immediately to the call of duty, the Brother, stopping at every table to ask the boys what their mothers had packed for lunch, hastened to the aid of the bully. Both boys were sent off to the office and order was restored to the cafeteria. Those were simpler days. Now the parents of the bully would probably sue the school for negligence. In those simpler days, however, the lesson was not lost on the 300 boys in the cafeteria that morning, and for the next few months the school bullies were incredibly cautious.

Fights suggest one minor aspect of the remarkably

competitive nature of the adolescent male. Boys can turn anything into a contest. If you're lucky, they turn school work into a contest. I've seen kids nearly come to blows over a tenth of a percentage point in a grade point average. They can turn work into a contest. Who has the fastest cleanup crew at McDonald's? They can turn cars into a contest, sometimes with tragic results, and of course, they can turn their relationship with their parents into a contest. How far can I get mom and dad to bend on this? To what limit can I push the curfew before they land on me? Whom do I ask first, mom or dad? Who is going to give me the better odds?

Thank God for sports and for extracurricular activities. A good bit of this competitive energy can be creatively channeled on the athletic field, on the stage or in the orchestra pit. You probably wouldn't be surprised at how quickly a playful shoving match in the hallways in an all boys' school can turn into a serious fight. You probably referee any number of contests between your children and can probably attest to the fact that sibling rivalry isn't the figment of some psychologist's imagination. Boys have to prove themselves, probably more to themselves than to anyone else. Often times they find good and proper ways to do this, such as getting good grades, excelling in athletics, getting and holding a good job, saving for something which is important to them. And often times they find improper ways such as fighting, driving recklessly, drinking excessively and tormenting their parents or their brothers and sisters. All of the examples above, positive and negative, are the means that a teenaged boy can use as he attempts to determine how he is to prove to himself and to others that he is a man.

In the movie, *The Bells of Saint Mary's*, Sister Mary Benedict, the principal of St. Mary's School, and Father O'Malley, the pastor of the parish, have a disagreement over a fight between two boys in the school yard. Father O'Malley applauds the school bully for his pugilistic skills much to the chagrin of Sister Benedict who has counseled the loser of the fight to turn the other cheek. Wise principal that she is, however, Sister Benedict realizes that Eddie (the loser) has to prove to himself that he can stand up to the bully. With a little help from Sister Benedict and a book on boxing, Eddie wins the next fight and then befriends the bully. I can't say I disagree with Sister Benedict's tactics in this instance. Not that I would encourage your son to fight!

You are probably asking yourself what kind of man is this who runs my son's school One month he may tell us that boys are usually obnoxious when they are sophomores, and the next month he tells us that they fight. Exactly! We have to understand the nature of the beast if we are ever going to help him in the difficult process of growing up. Thank God that your son is competitive. That drive will help him to make something of himself. Perhaps you could make a contest for yourself out of channeling your son's competitive nature and into paths that will make both of you proud. Think of the happy days you will spend at the beautiful retirement home in Florida that he is going to buy for you with his first million.

ON FINDING THE SAINTS IN YOUR LIFE

On November 1st, we celebrate the great Feast of All Saints, and as we celebrate that feast, we are reminded of the great saints of the Church: St. Francis Xavier, Sts. Peter and Paul, St. Teresa of Avila and St. Therese of Lisieux. While it's very important that we recall these great saints, I have always felt that the Feast of All Saints should be about the ordinary and unspectacular saints whom we have all encountered in our lives. I'd like to share with you some reflections on one of the "ordinary saints" who impacted my life.

Brother Myles McManus spent forty-eight years as a Xaverian Brother, and he taught until shortly before he died. While he taught religion and math, he was probably better known as a superlative track coach, and his nickname among the Brothers was Coach. Nobody ever called him Myles. It was always Coach.

Coach arrived at Xavier High School in Middletown in 1988 to work in the library and to teach a reduced schedule. Coach was definitely one of the great characters that the Xaverian Brothers have produced. He was a very simple and very humble man, but, like all of us, he had his quirks. Coach had struggled for many years with an addiction to alcohol until he discovered Alcoholics Anonymous. The last fifteen years of his life Coach was as sober as a judge and as devoted to Alcoholics Anonymous as he had previously been to alcohol. Nothing interfered with Coach's AA meetings.

Coach could be a principal's nightmare. An incredible procrastinator, he rarely corrected papers. This was apparently a lifelong habit, and there were stories that before he took his final vows, he was put under house arrest at the motherhouse in Baltimore because he had failed to write the monthly spiritual reflection papers which were required of all Brothers under temporary vows. Coach spent the summer at Mount St. Joseph wandering about and talking with all and sundry and never writing his reflection papers. When I began to get parental complaints that their sons didn't know how they were doing in math or religion, I ordered Coach to his room in the Brothers' house and told him he could not come out until I had from him corrected papers and grades. Of course, I had no authority to order Coach to his room, but, in his very humble way, Coach trotted off without a word and three hours later handed me a pile of corrected papers with the comment, "I don't know what they're worried about. I never give low grades, and the boys always do well." He was right about never giving low grades. As I thumbed through the stack of papers, I couldn't find anything lower than an 85.

One evening during PTA as I was wandering about the school building to make sure that there were no major difficulties, I discovered Coach sitting in his classroom in a circle with twelve men. I called him to the door and asked him what was going on. "These guys are the kids' fathers who are in AA with me. They didn't know I was a Brother because it's anonymous, you know, at AA. We're having a little AA meeting." When I suggested that perhaps some of the parents might want to talk to him about their sons' progress, he gave me his usual reply, "Nobody wants to see me. I teach the bright kids, and they all do well." With that he went back to his AA meeting, and I left shaking my head.

Coach and I left Connecticut together in 1991. He had an opportunity to return to his beloved Malden Catholic High School in Massachusetts, but I think his decision to leave Connecticut was more complicated than simply returning to a favorite former school. One of Coach's "old boys," Brother Lawrence Harvey, succeeded me as principal in Connecticut, and he and Coach were very close. Coach knew that he could be every principal's nightmare, and I suspect that Coach didn't want to be a burden to this young Brother as he took on the incredible responsibility of being a principal.

Three years later when Coach was dying of cancer, I went to see him at our retirement home in Massachusetts. Although the ravages of the disease had taken its toll on Coach, he spoke as if nothing were wrong until I got up to leave. At that point he said, "I need to thank you." I wondered quickly what he wanted to thank me for. Perhaps he was thinking of all the times that I covered for him as his principal, but it was far more simple than that. Everything with Coach was far more simple than you suspected. "I want to thank you for those pies." "What pies?" "A few years ago the Brother in the kitchen asked me what kind of cake I wanted for my birthday. I told him I didn't want cake. I wanted apple pies, and you made two beautiful apple pies for my birthday. I don't think I ever thanked you." Apparently covering for him as his principal was my job, but making pies for his birthday was a fraternal act of kindness that deserved gratitude. I left him that afternoon very grateful that he had come into my life. A few weeks later just before he died, Brother Lawrence Harvey visited him, and with the candor that had always existed between them, Larry asked, "Are you ready to go, Coach?" Coach replied, "All ready." I have no doubt that when Coach closed his eyes on this life, he opened them to see God face to face and that God smiled and said, "Welcome home, Coach."

Coach was a very simple and very humble man. While he struggled with his faults, he grasped very clearly Jesus' message "Love one another as I have loved you." He loved God. He loved his Brothers in religion, and he loved the thousands of boys whom God had entrusted to his care during his forty-year career in the classroom. The kids knew that he loved them, and they returned the compliment. I've heard many stories from Brothers who relate that, during Coach's drinking days, students and athletes would cover for him. They knew that he was on their side, and, in their adolescent way, they determined to be on his.

The Roman Catholic Church will never canonize Myles McManus. He was not the stuff of which canonized saints are made, but, in my humble opinion, he was a very saintly man. I suspect that if you look around your life, you'll discover a number of "ordinary saints," people, perhaps a grandmother or an uncle or a cherished friend, whose simplicity and care for others, even in the midst of their faults, touched you and made you a better person. As we celebrate this great Feast of All Saints, let's remember these ordinary, uncanonized saints who have peopled our lives. They are certainly in heaven with the great saints, and we can count on their prayers in heaven as we counted on their love on earth.

ON ADVENT AND PARENTING:
WAITING IN HOPE

Patience, people, till the Lord is come. See the farmer await the yield of the soil, He watches it in winter and in spring rain.
— From *Patience People* by John Foley, S.J.

Advent is perhaps the most beautiful season of the Church's liturgical year. The readings from *Isaiah* and the prophets of the Old Testament present eloquently the longing of the Jewish people for the Messiah, and the Church, as it prepares for the coming of Christ at Christmas, joins in that longing. Advent reminds us of how very much we need God and the salvation which God brings to us in Christ. If during Advent the Church waits, it waits in hope. The Church, and we as members of the Church, know that our God is a faithful god and that He will not disappoint us.

Parenting is a lot like Advent. Have you ever considered how much of your life as parents you spend waiting? When you first learned that you were to be parents, you waited patiently and perhaps anxiously through the nine months of gestation, hoping that your child would be born healthy. Once he was born, you waited patiently for his first words and his first steps. You waited for the "terrible twos" to pass and for the emerging signs of his personality. As he began his schooling, you waited for signs that he would adjust and that his schooling would go smoothly. As he began to develop his own life, you spent hours waiting in a car for Boy Scouts or Little League or soccer practice or piano lessons to come to an end so that you could take him home. As you waited, you hoped that all those things in which he was involved would help mold him into a person of whom both you and he could be proud.

Now that he's in high school, when he's out with his friends on a Friday or Saturday night, you wait, somewhat anxiously, to hear the sound of the car and his arrival home. You also wait for signs of maturity and for signs of independence. Perhaps at this point in his life you wait somewhat impatiently but still with the profound hope that the seeds you planted in him will come to fruition.

As the farmer waits patiently for the seeds he has planted to grow, so you wait for the seeds you have planted in your son to grow. As your son grows older, there are probably times when you wonder how well or how poorly you have done your job as a parent. It's at those times that you have to adopt an "Advent attitude." As you have waited through so much of your son's life, you have waited in hope, hope that your gifts as a parent will help him in his growth as a man and hope that your limitations as a parent will not hinder his growth. During Advent God reminds us that nothing is completely up to us. He reminds us that salvation is His gift and that His grace has a great deal to do with the molding of a young man. As you try to form your son into a mature and productive man, you have a tremendous partner in God.

The older I get, the more I realize how much depends on God and how little depends on me. This is particularly the case in my work with the young men at St. X. You and I, as parent and school teacher, plant seeds in the soil of our sons' and our students' lives; then we wait in hope. Parents and school teachers are like St. John the Baptist. We "make ready the way of the Lord." Let's pray together during Advent that all of the young men at St. X will become fertile ground for the seeds we have planted and that, with God's grace, they will mature into the men God wants them to be.

ON BEING SMART

When the seniors came in for their books at the beginning of the year, I asked one of them if his freshman brother was as smart as he. The senior wisely replied, "He's not book smart like I am, but in many ways he's far smarter than I." I thought that was an excellent response to a very stupid question. I'm the man who continually tells parents not to compare brothers because they are usually as different as night and day. While this letter might seem a bit more "stream of consciousness" than I usually write, I'd like to reflect with you a bit on "smartness" and the adolescent male and to reassure you that his adolescence is not necessarily an indicator of the man your son will become.

The senior recognized quite clearly that there are many ways to be smart. Schools, by their nature, tend to evaluate on "book smartness." St. X is quite proud of its Merit Scholars, its acceptances to highly selective colleges, the number of

Governor's Scholars it places every year and the significant scholarship money which our graduating class receives each year. Yet there are many boys at St. X who fit into none of those categories and who are as smart if not smarter than any number of our "book smart" students.

We have young men at St. X who can fix anything. They can disassemble, fix and reassemble a car, a computer or anything else mechanical in seconds. We have any number of young entrepreneurs who are running their own businesses, keeping the books and marketing their abilities to the local community. I was recently dumbfounded when one young man told me how much he made over the summer with the lawn care business he had started. I might add that some of the most successful St. X alumni I have met over the years are not the academic bright lights in their class. That's not to say that they aren't smart. We don't have any students at St. X who aren't smart! Smart, however, covers a wide range of talents and abilities.

Frequently, with a boy in trouble I'll use the rather sarcastic line, "You think that your smile and good looks are going to get you through life. Well, they won't!" Now there's some truth to that, but on another level it's not true at all. Personality, drive, the way a young man presents himself, common sense and insight are all factors in success. Life's greatest challenge for all of the young men at St. X is to find something that they are good at and to do it enthusiastically. It's a common thing for students these days to take more than four years in college and to change their majors three or four times. In some ways I think we have developed a society of "late bloomers," but that's not necessarily bad.

Over the years I have been dumbfounded by what some of my former students have accomplished. The boys who I thought wouldn't go far have gone much farther than I ever dreamed they would. One young man whom I had in senior English in the late 1970's is now a lawyer with a Ph.D.

in philosophy. I spent nine months trying to keep him awake. Another young man who drove me to distraction over the course of three years when I had him in Latin I, Latin II and Religion III is now a well-respected doctor. I was convinced that he was going to be on the FBI's ten most-wanted list. On the other hand, the smartest boy I ever taught failed out of an Ivy League college during his freshman year, losing a four-year scholarship. The last I heard he was a bartender on a riverboat on the Mississippi.

Boys are, in many ways, like cats. They have a remarkable facility for landing on their feet. What they are in high school is not always an indication of what they will become later in life. They mature, gaining new insight as they do. One of my former students is a professional actor. In high school he was the classic jock who had an incredibly low opinion of actors or anyone else in the arts. I reminded him of that at his tenth reunion from high school. He smiled and said, "Isn't life funny?"

I eventually met the brother of the senior I mentioned above. I asked him, "Are you as nice a kid as your brother?" He replied, "I'm not as smart as my brother." I, thank God, had learned my lesson and replied, "I didn't ask you if you were as smart as your brother. I asked you if you were as nice a kid as your brother." When he replied, "I think so," I told him that he would do just fine at St. X. I'll take a nice kid over a "book smart" kid any day of the week!

Don't despair if junior doesn't appear to be heading in a direction which you would like. Don't stop trying to influence him in very positive directions, but don't be discouraged if he insists on trying to find his own way. He'll probably land on his feet. And don't do anything so dumb as to compare brothers. As the senior pointed out to me, it's not a very smart thing to do.

ON OBFUSCATING THE TRUTH

One morning before school as I was sitting in the Driscoll Conference Room attending a committee meeting of the Board of Directors, I noticed a group of freshmen walking into the undergrowth behind the school garage. Anyone who has worked with adolescents for two minutes knows that these young men could be up to no good, so I excused myself from the meeting and went to investigate. The undergrowth behind the garage is rather dense, and at first I could not see the boys, but I could see clouds of smoke rising from the shrubbery. I bellowed, and they came out. When I asked them what they were doing, they told me they were simply talking. "Talking? You have to hide in the shrubs to talk?" They insisted that they were doing nothing untoward, and even when I mentioned the clouds of smoke, they denied vehemently that they had been smoking. I trooped them into the office, separated them and then did my best presidential, "One more lie out of your mouth, son, and you're out of here! Now tell me what you were doing." Without the moral support of their friends, each one admitted quite readily that he was smoking. Of course, I didn't tell them that I was relieved that it was cigarette smoke and nothing more serious.

Do kids lie? Is the sky blue? Is God good? If Richard Nixon only had the sense to employ a teenaged boy to concoct his Watergate story, the man would have ended his term in office without having to resign. To be fair though, kids don't really lie. They just obfuscate the truth. A detail inserted here, an essential element eliminated there, the truth is told but with a decided slant. The truth is slanted in proportion to the possible consequences of the truth's essential elements coming to light.

How often have I had a parent say to me, "But, Brother, my son said. . ." to which I have to reply, "Let me add a few missing facts." When a boy is sent by a teacher to the office, Brother Crane has the boy fill out a form on which he is to indicate why he was sent out of class. Later in the day the boy's teacher is asked to give his or her version of the incident. Believe me, any similarity between the two accounts is purely coincidental.

Please do not think that I approve of kids "slanting the truth." I certainly don't, and when I catch a kid in a lie, he knows very clearly how I feel. I'm not, however, surprised by the fact that kids lie. Adult memory can be rather short. I never told my parents all of the truth, and I'm pretty sure that you never told yours all of the truth. Should we tolerate kids lying to us? Definitely not. Should we be surprised when they do? No, again.

I am always very proud of a boy who tells me the truth immediately even though it is difficult to explain to him that telling the truth does not exonerate him from the consequences of his actions. In the past few years I have heard more and more frequently the argument: "How can you punish me when I admitted what I did?" The truth is what we as school teachers and as parents expect from our students and sons; however, we certainly would fail in our responsibilities if we trained our charges to believe that they have no responsibility for their actions beyond admitting that they did them. Life isn't like that, and life is the arena for which we are attempting to prepare them.

Here I need to add a rather touchy point which I hope won't offend you, but it's a point which I feel needs to be made. We have experienced more and more in recent years, parents lying to cover for their sons. It could be about an extra college visit day or an absence which shouldn't be excused. I need to tell you how discouraging I find that. We have very good reasons for all of our school rules and regulations, and those reasons are tested by time and experience. When a parent slants the truth a bit to get junior around one of our rules, junior obviously knows what the parent is doing. I don't think that is a lesson which parents want to teach their son. Again, I don't mean to offend, but as President of this school, I feel that I have to tell parents the truth.

Don't be surprised when you catch your son obfuscating the truth. It's the nature of the beast. Don't be surprised, but don't tolerate it either. Honesty isn't always easy, but it is still the hallmark of the mature man whom you and I hope your son will become.

ON MOTHERS AND SONS

Mary, His mother, pondered all these things in her heart. And Jesus grew in wisdom, age and grace before God and men.

—Luke: 251-52

In fourteen years of writing to parents, I've never once tackled the subject of mothers and sons. While I've quite comfortably written about the relationship between fathers and sons, I've wondered if I could do justice to that special bond which exists between a mother and her son. Rather than draw any conclusions, I would like to tell you some stories and let you draw your own conclusions. This letter will be a little longer than usual, but I think the subject deserves the space.

During my second year in the classroom, one of the boys in my freshman homeroom lost his mother during the year. My mentor, Brother Ivan, gave me explicit instructions to watch the boy carefully while his mother was dying and after her death. "To lose his mother while he's still a boy is one of the worst things that can happen to one of your students. A boy counts on his mother to love him no matter what, and losing her, he loses one of the great anchors in his life." With Brother Ivan's admonition in my mind, I watched the boy carefully, but I could not see what was going on inside of him. About a month after his mother's death, a group of my freshmen came to me before school and rather bluntly told me, "John stinks." I thought that there was an odd odor in the classroom, and during his class period I wandered by John's desk and discovered the truth of the boys' observation. When I told Brother Ivan about the problem, he replied, "He isn't changing his underwear. His mother made sure he did that. Call his father and tell him that you're sorry for his trouble, but he's got to snap out of it and start taking care of his son." Now the boy's father was probably forty, and I was twenty-five. Brother Ivan might have been able to carry that off, but I certainly wasn't. I called the man and mumbled something about dirty underwear. The father, probably unaware of my age, replied, "Brother; I don't know what to do. I never realized how much my wife held things together, and now, without her, I find it almost overwhelming. I can't think what to do." Overwhelmed as he was, he managed to deal with the underwear problem. About a year and a half later John came to me to tell me that his father was going to remarry. When I asked him how he felt about that, he replied, "Well, she's all right, but if she thinks she's going to replace my mother, she's dead wrong!" Then with a bit of the sophomore twinkle in his eye he added, "I'll have to say this. She's certainly good for my father's morale." Fortunately John came to love and respect his stepmother very much, but I think he was quite right when he realized that she would never replace his own mother.

I've discovered over the years that, in the unfortunate time when families are experiencing divorce, a boy will almost instinctively move to protect his mother, no matter how close he is to his father. I recall once an incredible fight breaking out between a father and his son at a track meet, and when I separated them and asked the boy what was going on, he almost spat the words at me, "He knows my mother always comes to my track meets, and he brought his girlfriend. I won't let him humiliate my mother like that." At this point the mother arrived on the scene, told her son that she could fight her own battles and made him go apologize to his father. When he went somewhat grudgingly, she turned to me and said, "I'm a lot stronger than he thinks I am, and I am touched that he would want to help me fight my battles. Of course I can't let him do that."

We have a good number of single-parent families at St. X where the mother is the sole support of the son. I've been impressed more times than I can mention by the concern that sons have for their mothers in these situations. The faculty alerted me once that one young man was about to leave St. X for financial reasons. I called the boy in and asked him what the problem was. He said. "It's just my mother and me, and I know how much she worries about paying my tuition. I don't want her to have to worry. I thought if I went to public school it would help." When I asked him if he wanted to stay at St. X, he said that he did but that it wasn't worth it if it caused his mother to worry. With the boy's permission I met with his mother, and we devised a plan that she could handle without significant worry. She was as concerned about him as he was about her. "He's only a boy, Brother, and I don't think he should be worrying about things that I should be able to handle." Their mutual concern for one another touched me very deeply.

Unfortunately, the mother-son bond can also be a cause

of great pain. Once I was standing in the hallway with Ms. Norris, the Director of our Guidance Department, and a boy whom we both knew passed and said hello. After he had gone, I asked Ms. Norris if she knew why he always looked so sad. She replied matter-of-factly, "He's about twelfth on his mother's list of priorities, and he knows it." I remembered Brother Ivan's words, "His mother is the one a boy counts on to love him no matter what," and I thought what a sad thing it must be for a boy who can't count on that.

Many of our retreat closings blend together in my mind, but I remember one where a junior got up to give his reaction and said, "Just before I left on retreat, I had a huge fight with my mother, and I said a lot of things that I didn't mean because I was angry. I'm glad my mom is here so I can tell her how much I love her and how sorry I am that I do stupid things that hurt her. After all, she's the only mom I've got."

That testimony is so eloquent that I won't even attempt to embellish it. Of course, Brother Ivan was right in the advice he gave me so many years ago. Fight with you though he may, Mom, your son counts on you to love him no matter what. Since he is a typical adolescent male, he doesn't tell you that. Please believe me when I tell you that it's true, and it will continue to be true long after your son has left his adolescence behind.

ON SPEAKING RESPECTFULLY

Once, in a burst of pious fervor, I volunteered to serve as a cook on a retreat which the Sisters of Mercy of Connecticut were sponsoring. My co-worker in the kitchen was a nun who had taught the first grade for forty years, and for the entire week, she spoke to me as if I were six years old. "Do we want to make our Jello now?" "We have to pay very careful attention to the time because we don't want our meatloaf to burn, do we?" "If you're really good, I'll let you lick the cake batter off the spatula." For the entire week, I replied with the appropriate "yes, no, or thank you, Sister."

While I found my interactions with the nun somewhat humorous, I recognized that I can do exactly the same thing. Since I was stationed in Connecticut for seventeen years, the last nine as principal, I had many opportunities to interact with men whom I had taught during my early years there. On one occasion I was speaking with the Board of the Alumni Association when a former student chided me, "Brother, I'm a physician with a wife and two kids. Do you think you could stop talking to me as if I were still sixteen years old?" Recognizing the validity of his complaint, I told him that I would try, but despite his education and his professional competence, I still saw the sixteen-year-old boy who sat in my classroom.

Both my encounter with the first grade nun and my former student's encounter with me reinforced in my mind how irritating it must be for adolescents when adults talk down to them. I know that this can be a flaw in school teachers, and I suspect that it can be a flaw in parents.

I have had my most success with teenaged males when I've tried to recognize and respect their need to be treated as young adults. At those times I remember the admonition in the old rule of the Xaverian Brothers which urges the Brothers always "To respect the man the boy will become." While I might not agree with what the young man is saying and while I might still refuse his request or send him to jug or tell him that he's out of line, I find things go much more smoothly when I speak respectfully and listen carefully. Things do not go smoothly when the young man pushes one of my buttons, and I begin to talk down to him, to belittle his experience or to dismiss him as "just a boy." Like most parents, I try to start by being reasonable, but there are certain things which I know will trump my best efforts. If a boy speaks back to me in a rude tone or gives me that "you poor, pitiful adult" look, all respect for his burgeoning independence is gone, and I launch into a tone and a style which do anything but respect "the man the boy will become."

Anyone who works with adolescents, parents or school teachers or bosses at McDonald's, will ultimately be driven occasionally to distraction by adolescent inconsideration or by adolescent failure to think of the consequences or by adolescent arrogance. Unless you are Jesus Christ or His Blessed Mother, it's just not possible always to be patient with or to understand an adolescent male. All that notwithstanding, the anonymous Brother who one hundred years ago wrote that it is always best "to respect the man the boy will become" was quite right. You always get farther with an adolescent when you respect him and when you do not belittle his experience simply because he is fifteen or sixteen years old. Just remember that respecting his experience and listening to him attentively does not mean that you have to agree or that you have to abrogate your parental responsibility to bring him back into line when he is out of line. It simply means that you try to remember how difficult it was to be an adolescent.

If you try to take this piece of advice from the President of your son's school, I have to warn you that you'll probably fail as many times as you'll succeed. At least that's been my experience in working with adolescents in the last quarter of a century. Perhaps, as we journey through Lent, you can take as your Lenten penance a renewed effort to be as patient with your son as you can be when he is being maddeningly adolescent. That's a far more difficult penance than giving up chocolate cake!

ON ADOLESCENT ATTORNEYS

I began my career in school administration as Dean of Discipline under the redoubtable Brother James Boyle. Brother James was a superb principal who taught me very carefully how to run a good school. No teenaged boy ever gave Brother James Boyle much grief. He had a withering stare and a rather sarcastic tongue which could stop the most recalcitrant of teenagers dead in his tracks. Whenever he was confronted by an aspiring lawyer, a young man who felt aggrieved and wanted to argue his case, Brother James would reply, "I'm not on trial here, young man. You are!"

You have no doubt discovered that most teenaged males are aspiring attorneys. They will argue with you about anything. Whether it be a school rule or one of your house rules or the color of the sky, a boy will argue to get around a rule or restriction, and many times he will simply argue for the sake of arguing. It's all part of the male-proving-you're-independent thing. Because it's a male thing, it normally tends to irritate fathers more than it does mothers. Mothers just sigh, and fathers (and school presidents) get their backs up.

You need to remember that every day your son attends school with 1500 other teenaged males. They are all aspiring attorneys, and they learn from each other those lines which are bound either to irritate parents or put them on the defensive. Because they have a ready resource in their classmates for new material, you have to resign yourself to the fact that, on many occasions, you will not be able to out-argue or out-reason your son. His arguments and his reasons for whatever it is he wants at the moment may be specious, but he will see to it that they are hard to refute.

Although there are times when you will not be able to out-argue or out-reason your son, you know in your heart what is best for him. While you might find that hard to explain, you are always best to go with your parental instincts and with your heart. You've lived with your son for fourteen or fifteen or eighteen years, and you know him better than he knows himself. Please never be afraid to be your son's parent. If your son is an aspiring attorney, you are the judge and jury. Attorneys don't always agree with the verdict handed down by the judge and jury, but the judge and jury have to do what is best for all concerned. I'd like to remind you here that whenever you call court into session to deal with your aspiring attorney, both mom and dad have to be in agreement. If mom is the judge, and junior can turn dad into the Supreme Court (or vice-versa), he'll do it. To continue my legal metaphor, don't be afraid to hold your son in "contempt of court." If he starts getting mouthy, always remember who's on trial!

As I told you in last month's newsletter, you always do well to listen carefully and to respond respectfully. There comes a point, however, when you have to play the judge to your son's aspiring attorney. Like your parents before you, your son will drive you to the point where your response will be,

"Because I'm your mother or your father, and I've lived longer than you. That's why!" That's not such a bad answer when you think about it. You have lived longer, and you are a lot wiser. More to the point, you do know him better than he knows himself, and you know what he needs. Don't ever let your son talk you out of your basic parental instincts!

I have had boys try to convince me that St. X should give up the dress code because the business world is becoming more casual. I've been told that we should drop our foreign language requirement because there are some very respectable colleges which no longer require the study of foreign language. I smile and give them the reasons, as I see them, why we won't drop the dress code or the language requirement. If they want to continue the argument, I smile and say, "Not while I'm President, son. Have a nice day." I do have a great comeback for those rare occasions when a boy will argue with me that St. X should become coed. I smile and remind the boy that if there are going to be 700 girls here, there will be 700 fewer boys. I then ask if he would like to volunteer to be one of the 700 fewer. That usually ends the argument.

When your son goes into his aspiring attorney routine, remember that you are the judge and the jury. Don't forget that, and don't be afraid to use your judicial powers. I'm firmly convinced that when you stand before God at the end of your life for the final judgment, He's going to note that you raised a teenaged male and give you at least a thousand-year credit on Purgatory. In the end, your son will be better than a plenary indulgence!

ON BEING UNUSUALLY BLUNT

In May, Dr. Sangalli and I both received a copy of the *Principal's Newsletter* from Mount St. Joseph High School in Baltimore. The Principal of the Mount, Barry Fitzpatrick, is a member of the St. Xavier Board of Directors and is an old friend both of mine and Dr. Sangalli's. Barry and I attended Catholic University together in the rather tumultuous late 1960's. When Dr. Sangalli and I read Mr. Fitzpatrick's letter, we were both struck by how courageous a stance he was taking with the parents at the Mount. It is a stance that I am sure is not universally applauded. As I read the letter, I became aware of my own lack of courage. I have written such a letter before but have not had the courage to send it. The topic of Mr. Fitzpatrick's letter is the problem of parentally sponsored parties at which alcohol is served. I would like to quote a paragraph of his letter:

"In my experience, I have often had parents tell me

that their sons are angry with them because they will not allow alcohol at a party for their son's friends in their home. I have never had a parent call me to ask what I thought about letting them drink but taking their car keys so they won't drink and drive. I have had parents tell me that supervising the teens drinking and seeing to it that they don't drive is the responsible thing to do. Let me say, unequivocally, that you cannot allow underage kids to drink at a teen party at your home and expect the understanding of this school. You should not expect the respect of your son, either, and never use the word, RESPONSIBLE, in the same breath as you explain away violating the law. Your son may like you for awhile, and his friends may think you are cool for a time, but ultimately the hollowlessness of it all will ring true. We cannot, as adults, continue to enable inappropriate behavior in this regard for the coming generations. We owe them better than that. Our students are at an age where, developmentally, they seek more and more to self-determine and to break away from what have become their accustomed imposed limitations, and they do this occasionally with little or no attention being paid to being responsible. Because of our own experience, some of us adults regard experimentation with alcohol before it is legal as a right of passage, excused with a sort of 'boys will be boys' attitude. Again, we owe them better than that. Being honest when it comes to teen drinking and their use of drugs requires, in some cases, that we adults examine our own behavior in this regard with an eye towards change. Doing the right thing is the goal here, not being popular, even for the moment. It is time for us adults to stop the nonsense, to be-

> come accountable for our own actions, and to see
> to it that we demand nothing less than responsible
> behavior on the part of those whose care is entrusted
> to us. We owe our sons nothing less!"

Strong words! True words! Now let me be rather blunt in my own words. A few months ago I told you that I found it incredibly discouraging that parents would lie for their sons to circumvent school rules. Well, that's only the tip of the iceberg. What I find most discouraging is parents who are more concerned with being their son's friend than they are concerned with being his parents. If you can manage being both your son's friend and your son's parent, you are indeed blessed, but if you can't carry off being both his friend and his parent, you have to be his parent first. He doesn't need any more friends. He needs you to be a guiding force, a parental force, an indicator in his life of where the boundaries are and of what is right and what is wrong. The media and the society will tell your son that everything is gray and that everything is up for grabs. As his parent, you owe him better than that. When he's out of line, you need to bring him back into line without worrying about whether he likes you or not or whether his friends think you are cool or not. Your son may not appreciate the stance you are taking now, but believe me, he will appreciate it as he grows older and realizes what you have done for him. You'll also be teaching him how to be a good parent when the time comes.

I write to you not because I feel that the vast majority of St. X parents are irresponsible in their child rearing. Quite the opposite. I find most St. X parents have a great deal of common sense in their approach to raising their sons, but I must admit that I see a growing trend every year among our parents to shrink from the responsibilities that they assumed with parenthood. Although I have no children of my own, I am very well aware of the challenges and problems in raising a teenager in this modern world. I live with them every day, and I see in myself, at times a tendency to tolerate things that I would never have tolerated a few years ago. Like the ocean wears down the rocks, teenagers can wear down adult stamina. Mr. Fitzpatrick's letter was a wake up call for me, and I hope it is a wake up call for you. There are certain things that St. Xavier High School is just not going to tolerate. There are certain behaviors in your son that you, as a parent, shouldn't tolerate either.

I can't tell you how frequently I hear from alumni at reunions that they are incredibly grateful to St. X for holding the line with them during their adolescent years. They may have hated it while they were enduring it, but as adults, they understand what the school was trying to do. Trust that your son will feel the same way. He may not like you while he's going through it but always remember that "like" has nothing to do with love. In the end, he will love you for putting him on the right path.

I realize that in writing rather bluntly I risk sounding like a cranky middle aged celibate out of touch with the modern world. If you read what I write to you monthly, I trust that you realize that I am not at all out of touch with teenaged boys and with the problems which teenaged boys face and which teenaged boys can create. While different in tone, this letter's purpose is to do what I do every month, to support you as parents in the very difficult but rewarding task of raising a teenaged son.

When I was interviewing to be the President of St. X, I was the only Brother among three candidates. As part of the interview process, I met with the Student Council who asked if I would make the school more democratic and give students more voice in school policy. I thought the requests were rather outrageous, but I was interviewing for a job, and I wasn't sure how much the Student Council had to say. I told them that I would always listen to them and that, while they might not always agree with my decisions, I would always do what I thought was best for them. I also pointed out politely that schools are not democracies. When they met with Brother Edward, the Principal at the time, he asked them about their interviews with the candidates. They told him that they wanted the Brother. When he asked them why, they said, "Because he sounded like a Brother." They meant it as a compliment. I took it as a compliment. Boys expect you to make them toe the line. In fact, they are rather surprised when you don't. Just a bit of advice from a cranky middle aged celibate.

ON REMEMBERING YOUR ADOLESCENCE

Today, on the feast of Our Lady's Assumption, I wrote the first two of my letters to parents of this school year. You will receive the second of these letters in the September mailing. If you were students in my British Literature course, I would tell you that the two letters are a perfect example of Blake's Doctrine of Contraries, two different aspects of one reality which may appear contradictory but which in reality are not. I say this now because I want you to keep in mind when you read the September letter that it was written on the same day as what you will read below.

This summer I discovered for the first time the novels of Chaim Potok and I was particularly struck by a quote from Karl Menninger which Potok uses as the epigraph for his novel *The Chosen*. Menninger says:

When a trout rising to a fly gets hooked on a line and finds himself unable to swim about freely, he begins a fight which results in struggles and splashes and sometimes an escape. Often, of course, the situation is too tough for him.

In the same way the human being struggles with his environment and with the hooks that catch him. Sometimes he masters his difficulties; sometimes they are too much for him. His struggles are all that the world sees, and it naturally misunderstands them. It is hard for a free fish to understand what is happening to a hooked one.

At one time or another, perhaps at many times in our lives, we have been hooked, and we have had the sad experience of having our struggles misunderstood by those around us. But far sadder than being misunderstood is the all too human experience of forgetting, when we have been freed from the hook, what it was like to struggle with the hook that had snared us. Compassion would be an easy virtue if we didn't have such short memories. How often in my own life have I met a student or one of my Brothers in religion who is struggling with a hook that has caught him, and I, with my short memory, forget my own past struggles and misunderstand what is going on in my student's or my Brother's life.

At times parents' and school teachers' memories are very short. We forget what adolescence was like and how painful it was to grow up. It is so easy to forget. The process of growing up is something that your sons have to face in many respects on their own. There is very little that you or I can do to make it easier for them. We can, however, remember and try to understand. Understanding your adolescent son won't ever be easy.

Your attempts at understanding may be as painful to you as his adolescence is painful to him, but in your attempts to understand him, no matter how fumbling they may be, he will experience your love. A boy who is convinced that he is loved is more than ready to deal with the hooks which may snare him in life.

"It is hard for a free fish to understand what is happening to a hooked one." In all our dealings with the people He sends into our lives, may the good Lord grant us long memories and compassionate hearts.

ON LIVING WITH THE CONSEQUENCES

School is about growing up and learning to take on responsibility. Hopefully, when a young man finishes his schooling and faces the world, he is able to face it on his own and to take responsibility for his life and actions. Teaching your son responsibility is one of our chief tasks at Xavier. When he does not live up to his responsibilities, he faces the consequences which his actions and decisions have brought upon him. In the counseling field there's a new philosophy called "Tough Love" which proposes that if a human being is going to mature, he or she must not be allowed to avoid the consequences of his or her actions but must learn to face them even when the consequences are not pleasant. Even before it had a name, we were functioning under this philosophy at Xavier. I've often told kids whom I might be punishing for this or that offense that I'm punishing them because I love them and because I think they have a lesson to learn. Now they don't always buy my reasoning at the time, but in most cases, with time, a boy will recognize that what you did was for his good, that what you did was, in fact, an act of love. One of my old nun friends, who had been a principal for years, once told me that expelling a boy from school might be the greatest act of love I could perform for him because it may just make him face himself for the first time.

Right now, you're saying to yourself, "What's the point, Brother?" The point is "as for schools so for parents." Parents and school have to join together in helping a boy mature in his sense of responsibility. When a boy is in difficulty and the parents are called in, the parents are obviously concerned that the school act fairly as regards their son. Teachers and school administrators can make mistakes since they are human, but in my experience ninety-five times out of one hundred the school is on target, and the boy is not. When a boy is in difficulty, I usually begin by asking parents, "What's your son's responsibility in all this?" If he's failing, did he ever show you his tests and quizzes? Did he seek help, not just once or twice but as long as he was struggling with the subject? If he has chosen to dispense himself from school regulations, was he unaware of the school's policy? Did he not know the consequences of being caught? By now, you sense my frustration. Dealing with the student population of a large boys' school is not a piece of cake. We have to be rigorous in our enforcement of school regulations, while at the same time we attempt to act always in a loving manner. Sometimes love is tough. The point of all this is quite simple: please let your son fight his own battles. Support him and love him but let him face the consequences of what he has done. The consequences may be an honor card or summer school. They were his actions; let them be his consequences.

Believe it or not, I was once taken to task by a man because I lodged a complaint with his twenty-five year old son's employer about a job the young man had not done well and for which I was paying. The son, thank God, had the good sense to be terribly embarrassed. What better time to learn responsibility than adolescence. It prepares for a lifetime.

ON SEARCHING FOR MEANING

In his book, *Man's Search for Meaning,* Victor Frankl, reflecting on his experience as a prisoner in Auschwitz during the Nazi's persecution of the Jewish people, writes:

> A human being is not one thing among others; *things* determine each other, but *man* is ultimately self determining. What he becomes—within the limits of endowment and environment—he has made out of himself. In the concentration camps, for example, in this living laboratory and on this testing ground, we watched and witnessed some of our comrades behave like swine while others behaved like saints. Man has both potentialities within himself; which one is actualized depends on decisions but not on conditions.

I taught *Man's Search for Meaning* for years in senior religion, and I still reread it frequently because Frankl so eloquently reminds me that responsibility for my life is mine and mine alone. I may not be able to control all of the things which may happen to me, but I can control my attitude towards the events and occurrences of my life. Frankl calls this the last of the human freedoms, "to choose one's attitude in any given set of circumstances, to choose one's own way."

I don't really know how analogous a marriage commitment is to a commitment to religious life, but I find that after nineteen years, the living out of my religious vows has definitely not become easier with practice. I suspect it might be the same with marriage. How I handle the difficult times and the adverse circumstances of my life and commitments is, Frankl maintains, the challenge which life offers me. My response to this challenge is my choice and mine alone.

There is many a day when I say, "Why me, Lord?" and when I wonder why I ever decided to become a religious who works with adolescents. The frustration is as real as are the questions. At those times I try to remember my friend Frankl and his challenge, and I pray that the Good Lord will give me the wisdom and insight to meet the challenge.

ON BECOMING YOUR PARENTS

You perhaps remember the great GEORGE M debacle. Last year a group of Xavier and Mercy students, all members of the cast of the schools' spring musical GEORGE M, decided to rent a motel room for an after-play party. Sister Mary and I discovered this and, anticipating the possible results of such a party, put an immediate kibosh on the revelers' plans. Shortly thereafter one of the boys involved, rather upset with the stance I took regarding the renting of motel rooms, came to see me. He said, "I hope that when I have children of my own, I'm not like you and my father. I hope I trust my children." As I attempted to respond to the lad, the thought occurred to me that I did indeed sound just like my father. I was using the same tone and the same arguments that had so irritated me when I was a teenager.

Not long ago a mother came to see me to discuss her son. I thought she was being most reasonable with the boy. She, however, was upset not so much at what her son had done but because, as she said, "I've become my mother. I never wanted to be like my mother. My son has turned me into my mother."

Time and experience have a funny way of changing our perspective on life. It is almost unavoidable that as adults we become our parents. So much of what we failed to understand as adolescents makes eminent sense to us now, and, while we might attempt to take a more enlightened approach to child rearing than our parents took, the nature of adolescence has not changed drastically. Kids can still drive us to the same distraction to which we drove our parents, and we respond with that same exasperation which so irritated us in our parents years ago.

Most of the time we try to be reasonable with our kids. Kids, however, don't have the perspective of our experience, and they can think we are being unreasonable. When we have been as reasonable as we can, and after that, we still get the "Why?" and the "you poor, old-fashioned fool" look which adolescents love to give adults, we are all eventually driven to "Because I'm your mother (or your father or your principal) and I said so!" History does have a way of repeating itself, doesn't it?

Not to worry. There is a just God and twenty years from now your son's children will be driving him to the same distraction to which he is now driving you. Think of the fun you'll have being an indulgent grandparent as you watch your son become yourself!

ON THE SCHOOL OF HARD KNOCKS

At a recent alumni reunion I was talking with a young Xavier grad who had just finished his first year in the world of work. When I asked him how he liked working for a living after sixteen years of school, he replied, "Once I realized that the smile and the charm which had gotten me through twenty-two years of life weren't going to work with my boss or my customers and once I resigned myself to the fact that I was going to have to work for a living, things have been going along fine." This young man discovered rather quickly that charm and a smile are great provided there's a good bit of substance behind them.

At the risk of sounding like an educational dinosaur, I worry about the kids we have in school and their future. They have so much in the way of worldly goods, and they've worked so little to get them. Even more frightening is the fact that they don't realize how hard mom and dad have worked to provide them with the lifestyle to which they have become accustomed.

This is not to say that kids are necessarily lazy. I frequently hear glowing reports from the various employers of Xavier boys, but let's face it. Mom and Dad are still the major source of funding and a pretty generous source at that. What happens when Junior is thrown into the cold pool of life? Will he have the necessary skills to swim on his own?

The school of Hard Knocks is still the best educational institution going, and try as we might, you and I are not going to spare your son a term or two in that famous school. We can, however, help him to graduate successfully from Hard Knocks Academy by preparing him for the course of studies there.

Hard Knocks Course 101: Learning to Fight Your Own Battles

"My French teacher, Miss Francophile, hates me and that's why I'm doing so poorly, and Brother Geometricus is impossibly difficult. Absolutely everybody is failing math."

"I'm sure your French teacher doesn't hate you but, knowing and loving you as I do, I would be surprised if you haven't given her reason to dislike you. I'd suggest you straighten the whole situation out with her since you have to pass French. Too bad Brother Geometricus is tough. Life is tough and you're not everybody. If everybody is failing math, I suggest you be the exception."

Hard Knocks Course 102: Living With the Consequences

"We know it's July 15th, but, if you recall when you violated your curfew on July 1st, we said no car for a month. We said it; we mean it; see you on July 31st."

"I believe summer school is the result of failing. Summer school runs about $165.00. How do you suggest you're going to pay for it so you can return to school in September?"

"You're the one who got suspended from school for being rude to Miss Francophile. Too bad you have to wait until 5:30 for a ride home. No, I can't pick you up right after jug."

Hard Knocks Course 103: If It's Worth Having It's Worth a Little Sweat

"So you want to go on the school trip to Boca Raton. I see that Burger King is looking for help. If you start now, you may just have enough money by spring break. No, you can't ask grandma."

Having said all of the above, let me add (for your consolation and mine) that kids, like cats, seem to be able to land on their feet. The irresponsible boy has a way of becoming the responsible man. I've seen innumerable kids about whom I worried seriously become successful, hard working adults. Frequently they return to tell me how the school has gone to the dogs and how it just isn't as tough as it was when they were here. Both assumptions are untrue, but it's refreshing to hear from men who, when they were students at Xavier, showed all the signs of outdoing Peter Pan in never growing up.

Hopefully you and I proudly hold our diploma from the School of Hard Knocks although we may occasionally be forced into a refresher course. We should be well prepared to get junior ready for his inevitable stint in that prestigious academy. He might just thank us after he's graduated.

Are you ready to send him back to school yet?

ON LITTLE LEAGUE AND LINUS BLANKETS

Little League was pure torture. I was such a pathetic athlete that, whenever a "leftie" got up to bat, the coach pulled me with great flourish from my normal position in right field so that my atrocious fielding would do no permanent damage to the team's effort. Little League was one of those experiences that my parents thought would be good for me. Pure torture. Later I became the student manager of the athletic department at Marian High School. I was, in effect, the assistant A.D. I could organize the jocks; I just couldn't be one. Little League— how I hated my parents for making me go through the agony of it all. But then again, there are so many things I wouldn't be able to do today if my parents had let me have my way. I certainly wouldn't be able to swim, and I definitely wouldn't be able to ride a bike. I balked at both of those undertakings. And I most certainly wouldn't have three college degrees listed after my name. School work was a low priority in my life. It was high priority in my parents' lives, and it would no more have occurred to them to let me take the easy way out than it would have occurred to them to take a trip to the moon. My father's philosophy of education was incredibly simple: shut your mouth and do what the Sisters tell you. It's a good thing my father's philosophy prevailed over my laziness because I can read and write rather well today.

Kids naturally shy away from undertaking things which seem difficult to them or which might hold the possibility of failure. The need for security, which is so much a part of all of our lives, is particularly strong in the adolescent. Unfortunately, the adolescent doesn't usually see that at times security has to be abandoned in favor of growth. Throughout the ages (to add a universal perspective!), parents have been burning their children's "Linus Blankets" and pushing them out into life. Kids normally want to take the easy way out. Parents know that the easy way out is usually not the best way out. "Because I've lived longer" is not a bad reply to that (usually sarcastic) adolescent question, "What makes you think you know what's good for me?" Usually you do, and usually he doesn't. It's been the case as long as there have been parents and children.

How well I remember the day I graduated from college. My parents were far prouder of what I had accomplished than I was. They had a right to be. If they had let me have my way when I was a kid, there probably wouldn't have been a college degree. In not letting me take the easy way out, my parents were in good company. In the garden of Gethsemani on Holy Thursday night, Jesus asked His Father to "let this cup pass me by." God the Father said no. Jesus did what His Father wanted, and we have the joy of being redeemed. Remember that the next time you make your son do something that he considers "pure torture." If you're in God's company, you must be on the right track!

ON WALKING TIGHTROPES

This summer I read a recent best seller, *Less Than Zero*, by Brett Easton Ellis, a young college student. The book depicts rather graphically the life style of wealthy southern California teenagers, and I must admit I found the book incredibly disturbing. The alcohol and drug abuse and the sexual promiscuity described are very real elements in today's society and are certainly not confined to California. Xavier boys may not have the money that their counterparts in this book have, but they certainly have all the pressures and temptations which modern society presents. At times I feel that working with adolescents is like attempting to shovel sand against the tide. How can we possibly hope to have any effect on them when everywhere they look in today's world they see held out to them values that are at best unchristian and at worst inhuman? Television, books and magazines, music and videos all proclaim a "me first" pleasure principle that has little regard for the welfare of

206

others or even for personal growth and development.

How can I as a school teacher and you as parents counter these worthless values that are every day presented to your son by society as worthwhile values? I wish I had a pat answer, but I don't. I do think that communication is the key; however, communicating with an adolescent is far from easy. He certainly isn't going to bring up as dinner conversation the fact that "crack," the new inexpensive form of cocaine, has hit the Connecticut high school scene nor is he going to tell you that his best friend's girlfriend may be pregnant.

If your son is typical, he will fight any attempt you make to find out what is going on in his world. In his view you are hopelessly out of date with no true appreciation of the real world and, therefore, you have very little to offer in terms of providing a map through some of life's more tricky highways.

My best bet and yours is to keep talking to him even when he doesn't want to talk to us. We have to attempt to create an atmosphere in which he will feel comfortable talking to us when he feels the need. The key element in that atmosphere has to be love. He has to know that no matter what he tells you, it won't change your love for him. The noted psychologist Carl Rogers calls this "unconditional positive regard." We see it well exemplified in the approach Jesus took 2000 years ago to the woman caught in adultery, "Neither then do I condemn you. Go and sin no more." If that anonymous biblical woman had any more difficulties, you can be sure she would feel quite comfortable talking to Jesus of Nazareth.

A number of years ago, I was talking with a very troubled boy, attempting to get him to articulate his problem for me. I used my best Carl Rogers approach, assuring the boy that no matter how bad it was, I would still care for him. Carl Rogers worked, and the boy told me what he had done. Unfortunately the negative side of my Irish Catholic upbringing momentarily overwhelmed my attempts at dealing with the boy as Jesus would and I exclaimed, "Oh my

God, you didn't?" So much for unconditional positive regard and my non-judgmental posture.

Creating an atmosphere where adolescents will feel comfortable talking with us is no easy task for us adults, and it is further complicated by the fact that we, as parents and as school teachers, on occasions have to help them on their road to maturity. Translate "help them on their road to maturity" on the home front by: revoking driving privileges, establishing curfews, curtailing work hours or allowance, grounding, etc. Translate the same phrase on the school scene by: jugging, suspending, calling mom and dad to the principal's office, and at worst expelling. What a tightrope!! We have to let them know that they are loved at the same time that we have to help them grow up.

The parents in the novel I mentioned above had not a clue that their children were lonely and alienated, seeking support in a world that could only destroy them. Keep talking to your son, even if he doesn't talk back, and, in some small way, let him know every day that you love him. More than he needs anything else, he needs to know deep down in his gut that you love him and that there's nothing he can do, no matter how bad, that will make you stop loving him. If he knows only this, he can never go too far astray.

The adolescents in my best seller felt that they were worth "less than zero." You and I have to make sure your son knows that, as far as we are concerned and as far as God is concerned, he's worth more than the world.

ON BEING A CATHOLIC HIGH
SCHOOL PRINCIPAL

It was a dark and stormy night, and for reasons that I could not fathom, we had not called off a basketball game. In the wintry wind, Mr. Jaskot and I spread rock salt along the courtyard sidewalk. Ever conscious of the problem of liability and always without overtime maintenance help, which we can't afford, I set out to spread the rock salt. Mr. Jaskot felt sorry for me and came out to help. Through the wool face mask I was wearing I commented, "You can bet that the principal of Middletown High doesn't do this." Mr. Jaskot just laughed. Whether it be spreading rock salt or, my next favorite task, locking the school building and setting the security alarm at 1:00 a.m., a Catholic high school principal, particularly a religious one who has the misfortune of living right at the institution, can count on having to perform many tasks which public high school principals never even have to consider. I've swept

209

floors and washed windows at the last minute before a school activity because our ever understaffed maintenance crew couldn't get to them. I've moved staging and set up chairs— all to save a few pennies in an overly tight budget. Most Catholic high school principals would recognize the tasks listed above as "order of the day," but although they make up a good bit of a Catholic school principal's day, they certainly are not what it means to be a Catholic high school principal.

I have been most a Catholic high school principal on those occasions when I have sat with grieving parents who have just lost their son. I have been most a Catholic high school principal when, with Sister Mary, I have waited in the emergency room of the Middlesex Memorial Hospital pinch hitting for parents and hoping that they would arrive soon to tend to their injured children. I have been most a Catholic high school principal when I have arrived at the Middletown Police Station at 2:00 a.m. to deal with a Xavier boy who has gone afoul of the law and to calm his distraught parents. I have been most a Catholic high school principal when I have sat with boys whose lives seemed to be falling apart around them and who felt as if they had no one on whom they could depend. I have been most a Catholic high school principal when on Monday mornings I began everybody's week with my "fervorino" congratulating the kids for the good they had done and taking them to task for the not so good.

The security alarm wailing at 3:00 a.m., the sudden snow squall with maintenance nowhere in sight, the endless nights of locking the bloody building and the constant scrambling to make sure that there is enough money to meet the next pay-roll—all of these are minor inconveniences. The things that matter, the things that I will remember about my nine years as Xavier's principal, are the people, the members of the Xavier family with their joys and sorrows. It has been my privilege to walk with many of these families in some of the most difficult times of their lives. It has also been my privilege to walk with others in the joyous times. When I stand before the judgment seat of God and He reviews my years as principal of Xavier, I doubt He is going to ask me about the balance sheet or the state of the physical plant. I suspect He is going to ask me if I did my best to shepherd this little portion of His flock. In all humility I will be able to answer, "Yes, Lord, I did. At times it didn't seem good enough, but it was my best, and I did it with my whole heart."

ON BROTHER THOMAS MORE
AND GOLDEN ALUMNI

Brother Thomas More taught at St. X from 1940 until 1950, and in 1953 he returned as the Principal of the school. During his tenure as Principal (1953-1960), Brother Thomas More was instrumental in St. X's move from Broadway to the present campus. As I speak with St. X alumni from the "Thomas More era" I am repeatedly struck by the reverence which these men have for Brother Thomas More. It is not a hyperbole to say that they worship him.

In June I attended the 50th anniversary reunion of the Class of 1948. Brother Thomas More had taught all of the men of the class. I sat next to him at the head table and watched these men, all now in their late sixties, come to express their gratitude to Brother Thomas More for all that he had done for them. One gentleman literally knelt at Brother Thomas More's feet and said, "Brother Thomas More, you probably don't remember me, but you taught me German in 1947. One day you kept me after class and told me that I was becoming a thug and that I needed to get myself on the right path. You told me that if I could just get myself together I would have a very happy and productive life. Well, you were right. I was a thug, and the care you showed me on that day turned me around." He then went on to tell Brother Thomas More about his family and his life. Brother Thomas More listened attentively and thanked him for his gratitude. When Brother Thomas More spoke to the class that evening, they all listened with rapt attention, and when he finished they stood and applauded. These men obviously know what a wonderful thing it is to have your life touched by a good teacher. Brother Thomas More is eighty-two years old, and he doesn't like to stay out late. As soon as the speeches were over, he nodded to me that it was time to go. It took us a considerable time to get across the room as these golden alumni came over to their old teacher to shake his hand and to thank him for all that he had done for them. I was very touched by the events of the evening and proud to be in the presence of a Xaverian Brother who had such a profound effect on a group of teenaged boys over 50 years ago.

When Dr. Sangalli hires a new teacher, he brings the teacher in to me to give the new teacher a "pious pep talk" on St. X and Xaverian education. I tell all young teachers that we have no interest in hiring any teacher who looks upon teaching as a job. We want teachers who know that teaching is a vocation, a work to which God calls them. I tell young teachers that we expect them to challenge the boys academically and to hold them to rigorous academic and disciplinary standards. Yet all of the challenges and the rigor is a mere preparation for their work as Cthiolic educators. Once they've got the Tigers tamed, the real work begins, the work of their vocation as a teacher. Teenaged boys are the most forgiving creatures on God's earth, and they'll forgive a teacher anything as long as they know in their hearts that the teacher really cares for them. When Brother

Thomas More took that young man to task in 1947, the young man knew that it was love for him that motivated Brother Thomas More, and he responded to that love.

I hope and I pray that during his four years at St. X each young man encounters a few teachers like Brother Thomas More, teachers who can have a profound effect on his life. As I watch every day the interaction between the faculty and the student body, I know that my prayers have not gone unheard and that my hopes are every day realized at St. X. Whether it's Brother John standing at the "T" and joking with students as they arrive in the morning or Ms. Keene in the Retreat Office putting her retreat team together or Ms. Reisert attempting to raise the cultural level of the school by filling the hallways in the morning with her classical music, I see the spirit of Brother Thomas More alive at St. X every day.

In June, after school had ended, I got a tearful phone call from a mother who wanted to thank me and St. X for all the school had done for her son. Her son had a bumpy beginning during his freshman year which was made easier by the care and concern of Mr. Larkin in the Guidance Office. Mr. Higgins took up the cause during the boy's sophomore year, and Mr. Simms befriended him during his junior year. The mother was just incredibly grateful that so many people had paid attention to her son. She ended by saying, "Brother, you say that they'll be grateful to us years later when they realize what was given to them, but on graduation day, with his diploma in his hand, my son turned to me and said, "Thanks, mom, for sending me to St. X." You can imagine that phone call made my day, my week, and possibly even my year.

As I mentioned above, I hope and pray that during his four years at St. X your son meets a Brother Thomas More. Now the Brother Thomas More he meets may not be a Brother at all, but in our wonderful lay faculty your son will meet men and women in whom the Xaverian spirit is very much alive, men and women who view their work in the classroom and on the playing fields as a vocation, a call from God. At the meeting of the Board of Directors last May, the Educational Programs Committee asked a group of seniors what they knew about the Xaverian Brothers. They knew a great deal. One senior put it quite eloquently. He told the Board, "Many of us weren't taught by the Brothers who are here, but so many of our teachers are guys who graduated from St. X and who were trained by the Brothers. We learned about the Brothers through them." There are thirty-seven St. X graduates on our faculty, but they are not the only "bearers of the charism." All of our veteran teachers are beautiful examples of Xaverian teachers at work, and it's very heartening for me to see that spirit growing brighter every day in the younger men and women on our faculty.

As we begin the 134th year in St. X's history, please pray with me that the spirit of Brother Thomas More and of the Xaverian Brothers will remain alive and well at St. X, and please pray with me for the 1500 young men who will be educated at St. X this year. May each of them find his Brother Thomas More on the St. X faculty and may each of them become men of whom St. X can be proud.